How I Became
The Love of My Life

How I Became
The Love of My Life

Labris Willendorf

CONTENTS

Dedication

This is dedicated to my mother, Linda Marie Verdugo Sterk and family friend, Zakari Adams. Both were creative, broken, beautiful souls that left this Earth too soon. Their deaths inspire me to live my passion every day for myself and for those that can't.

This is for all the love my mom gave me in her own way, her encouragement as a child that I could do and be anything. She raised me to have pride in who I am. I am proud to be a curvy, queer, sassy, intelligent, adventurous lover of life.

I also write in honor of Zakari. Among many things, he was a photographer with an eye to see the tremendous in the ordinary. I am grateful to have known him, and strive to see the magic in everyday life, while I am lucky enough to be here.

Gratitudes

There are a lot of people I am grateful for, so this is a long list! I want to thank my sister for her love, encouragement and for us being each other's heroes. To both my sister and sister-in-law for challenging me to dig deeper into my pain and be brave enough to share it. To my Amazing Love, Shawna, thank you for encouraging me to not give up and to publish this myself. I'm also so grateful for your incredible art, you brought my vision to life on the cover. To Tiffany for giving me Andy's phone number and starting me on my path to writing my first book. Also, for her unwavering encouragement and enthusiasm for my book and my life. To Andy Couturier for help, encouragement and humor. You made writing class something to look forward to for years. To Cynthia Kingsberry for your fabulous editing skills and encouragement. To Molly for always being in my corner, letting me know I should use commas, and where I had them hidden the whole time. To the rest of my friends and family who have believed in my creativity, growth and passion. I wouldn't be doing this without everyone I have listed. Last, and definite not the least, to you, the reader, I appreciate your time and money spent on giving my book a chance!

A Note for the Reader

So, how did I actually become the love of my life? Laying on my bed, one leg propped up on the other, I look at my chipped burnt orange toenail polish and grin. These size 7 ½'s have carried me on many journeys during my time walking here. Looking at my legs, my calf muscles pronounced under my white skin and dark stubble, it's winter and I wear leggings so why shave? My glance then rests on my left fleshy thigh and the dancing fairy tattoo. I called her my alter ego once but she's me now. My chocolate eyes look at her free hands over her head, dancing to the purple music notes in pink high heels, short skirt and corset with a Taurus symbol tattoo on her leg. I love that my tattoo has a tattoo! I smile every time I get to see her. From here I reach my stomach and after decades I finely cherish this part of me. I have embraced all of my body's bodacious curves. I then stop at my heart because it is what has led me all this way. Beneath my surface, the bones and blood, my inner higher self has been my guide through all of this and so that is where I begin my story.

I had reached the bottom of my self so the only direction I had left to go was up.

The devastation that I couldn't handle, I channeled into righteous anger which is what propelled me into my new life. I had no idea I was capable of rage or that it could create a bravery that would lead me through to such revolving joy. In my darkest time I remembered that I was there. I found myself again and realized I had been buried under someone else's expectations, but I was still there.

I am writing this because I want you, who is reading this, to know that the biggest fear you have, the biggest pain or sadness can be given so much adoration and compassion by you, alone that you can turn it around. You can and make it something to honor yourself for. I am not saying this is easy, being courageous never is, but I promise, you are worth it. When the pain breaks you open to all of its jagged surfaces and that all too familiar horrible taste of the unknown is cold against your tongue, it is here you aren't just open to tragedy, you are wide and free to take in the pouring of life's juices. Here you are Everything you can be. In your vastness, you can allow a new lover's nectar to glide down your neck or a forgotten city's secrets to seep into your elbows. A dear friend's giggles can guide you as you learn to be your own knight in occasionally polished armor.

I am also writing this because I read a book that made me feel not so alone when my soul was sprawled out. I exposed myself to this new life that I had no idea how to begin. All I knew was that it had to be better than what I had left. The author in that book was writing about the same feelings, she felt what I felt, knew exactly what I was going through. In reality hers was of course a different journey, but I felt a connection.

My goal is to be that connection for you, if you choose. Vulnerability is what we all are drawn to. If someone opens up to us, shows us all of their things they would rather keep hide, there is a trust that forms. I am willing to expose suppressed treasures, some sparkly and some that didn't feel like gems in the moment. If my book isn't your thing, no problem. I encourage you to keep up the search. I hope whatever book you make a connection with, because the one I found made me smile every time I read it and sometimes that was the only time in a day a smile would cross my face. When you are in tears, rocking back and forth alone on your bed, I don't want you to feel lonely. You are the only one that feels the way you do in that moment but please don't feel abandoned. Know that you are loved, love is at the core of us all, and we are all joined so even if you don't believe, it's happening anyways. When you have bloodied your fingernails trying to crawl your way out of the suffering and after the salty droplets have run past your chin, listen to a song that helps you get your ass out of that bed and dance even if only for the chorus. Know that the kisses you might miss are still squishy in your soul. Accept it all, the angst, glory and the escapades. You might be thinking what does she know, but I've done it and that is exactly how I know that your life can be all that you desire. Whatever it is that you have yearned for, only you can make that far off thought your reality. Believing in yourself is the first step. I realize it sounds like the hokiest thing, but I know it to be true.

While you read the intimate details of my life that some of my friends don't even know, in exposing myself I hope to be your silent witness. I aspire to be a friend that just gets you without any explanation. So, here we are and I welcome you to share in my layered pain, crooked laughter, moaning orgasms and uncompromising positivity. Shall we?

4

Walking the Camino de Santiago

I looked down to my right at the makeshift memorial for the people who had died doing what I was about to attempt. As I stood on the concrete path where it dissolved into uncovered earth, my feet began to sweat. They were used to being in my purple hiking shoes with each toe in their own compartment of my special black "toe socks." It wasn't about the walking. I didn't realize I was holding my breath in my raspberry puffy coat, matching rain jacket and waterproof grey pants. When I remembered to inhale, the chilly French air reminded me it was early morning the day after Easter. I was surrounded by other people and mountains protruding from the Earth but I was only able to stare at the dying flowers, notes from loved ones and the small rock formations built by human hands. I asked myself, "Who were these people and why did they come here? Why did they risk their lives to be a peregrino, a pilgrim on The Camino de Santiago?"

I didn't know their answers. What I knew was that walking 500 miles, up and down the Pyrenees Mountains from France and through Spain was the only thing that made sense to me after leaving my marriage and fourteen year relationship. This was more than a spiritual pilgrimage, it was a path leading me back to me. I needed to remember the woman I had been before my marriage and unearth who I was becoming after. Walking The Camino was my only answer. I was relearning to listen to my gut and what she said was, "It is only this Now."

That being said, not all of me was strong in the conviction of The Camino. The familiar fear creature wanted desperately to crawl up from my skittish stomach and cling on my elusive heart. I chose to not allow it any access. I had dedicated six months training to do this. I joined a gym that was filled with muscly body builders and spent my evenings after work on the elliptical, one mile, three miles, five miles. One Wednesday the month before my pilgrimage I got up to nine miles. My weekends were spent run/walking 5ks, 10ks and hiking in the forest. My longest hike was fifteen miles two weekends before I left.

Besides the exercising, I had so many trips to my favorite outdoor store I felt like people would soon start calling me Norm like in the 80's TV series Cheers. One of the most joyful parts of the preparation was being able to pick out the gear. I had so much fun trying on lightweight pants, checking shirt labels for sunscreen and bug repellant fabric. I even found travel panties that were made of quick drying material... with lace! My water reservoir was next but the most important, the backpack. The brand was Gregory and was made especially to fit women's bodies. The moment I put it on, I knew it was perfect; earthy green, cushy shoulder, hip straps and the right amount of pockets.

With all of the training, unbeknownst to myself I slowly evolved into an athletic person. As a chubby little girl with asthma I had not experienced the euphoria that came with my endorphins and the pride of achieving a goal: getting my time from a fifteen minute mile to my personal best of eleven minutes twenty seconds. With the knowledge, gear and practice, I began to realize I could actually walk 15-20 miles per day. In April of 2014 I was ready for the journey. I had paused my American life for 6 weeks in exchange for a backpack and travel guide. I was not about to let my all too familiar fear turn me back.

"You've got this, let's go." I jogged to join up with my friend Matt on the path that disappeared up into the unknown. The daunting thoughts of the memorial were left behind as the next 6 hours I hiked with more conviction and devotion to anything I had ever physically done. My body carried me through frozen liquid, falling water and lime green grasses sprinkled with white sheep. I went up, and up and up. One foot in front of the other, breathing with the melody of the left, right, left, right, left, right.

Now, you might be wondering, how did I even know about The Camino de Santiago? It is one of the most well-known and well-traveled pilgrimages in the world. The Way of St. James, as it is also called is dedicated to one of Jesus' apostles. I am not even religious so it didn't make sense to me either. My friend Hanna's husband Matt walked the Way in 2007 and that's where I first heard of it before I went to see the movie, "The Way," in September of 2011. I was unhappy in my marriage, and while watching the movie I cried, knowing that somehow I would walk it but not with my wife. The combination of the characters of the movie, the scenery and the story drew me to Spain. When I had no idea what to do with my life, I remembered the movie and knew that's where I needed to be.

An obstacle before I left: "Must be nice to get six weeks off." None of my close friends or family actually said this to me but I had guilt and shame for asking for the time. Later it dawned on me: I felt like I didn't deserve it. Why should I be able to have all that time to walk through Spain to go on an adventure of my choosing? Well, because I was alive and deserved it just like everyone else. We have so few moments on this beautiful blue planet, why be miserable? Why let others influence your glee? If others are unhappy about your adventurous ways, that's on them. Their negativity is harder on them than you. In the past I'd let people's opinions make me feel guilt or shame. As I worked on my self-worth I began to realize that my battles are no one else's and vice versa. If I'm enjoying myself and not harming anyone then I'm great! Once I let go of all of that, I found that everyone was delighted for me. I had no idea what or who I would find on the mud filled roads, cobblestone bridges or empty fields. I had hopes that at least one person would be me. I didn't care what I faced; I knew The Camino was what I needed.

The day after Easter in 2014 I said to myself, "I saw this in a movie, I saw this and now I'm doing it." I said this as I left the small town of Saint Jean, France and I stepped onto the road that would lead me to the Pyrenees Mountains. I glanced to the left and noticed the first official marker and I smiled. I stood there next to Matt and the bright blue sign with the yellow shell marker. I had come this far and I would only go forward.

The first day of hiking was all up. I was elated to see the refugio where I'd spend my first night on the Camino. That first night there was a great sense of comradery. There were three long tables that we sat around, introducing ourselves as we passed baskets of bread and carafes of Spanish red wine. The American mother and daughter were quite a pair, wondering how they would get along, as the daughter invited her mother only after a friend backed out. There were a few women, one Australian and more Americans walking it alone, along with a single young Brazilian man who was writing a book about The Camino and an older Canadian couple. It was not a late night as we were all up early because they were kicking us out at 7am.

The accommodations fit six people to a room, in bunk beds. I felt lucky to have two of the other five people be my friends, Hannah and Matt. The other three were the young Brazilian man and unfortunately the sweet Canadian couple with the wife that snored like a mack truck honking underneath my head. I was in the upper bunk with my face inches away from the ceiling and my body wrapped in my sleeping bag liner as I had been warned about bedbugs. A few hours later, wrapped in the liner and complete darkness, I woke in a full blown panic attack.

If you have never had one I envy you. I wouldn't wish them even on a person I despised. The first time I experienced one I felt like I was going to die if I didn't take off all of my clothes and run outside. Panic attacks had become a reoccurrence after leaving my marriage and I would wake up in the middle of one. I thought I had worked through my anxiety but there I was silently gasping in the fear of being trapped. I was literally locked in the refugio, and tried not to let that fact enter my consciousness. I made my way down the five step ladder, out the bedroom door and into one of the two bathrooms for the thirty of us. I remember the cool porcelain of the toilet against my sweaty thighs, holding myself into a fake comfort, telling myself I only had to make it through fifteen minutes and it would be over. I concentrated on my breathing; in and out, in and out. I washed my face, no paper towels to dry but that was the least of my concerns. I made it back to my room, trying not to observe the locked chain on the front door. As I crawled into my bunk, the heat and night noises of strangers surrounding me, I promised myself I would not ever do that again. I promised that if I was strong enough to make it the rest of the night and sleep so I could walk into Spain and to a hotel, I would only stay in a place that I could sleep in alone.

The next morning I was so relieved to have gone back to sleep and see the sun rise over the mountains. There was a bit more uphill but at the point right before the most intense downhill everyone was tightening their laces. I was told you could lose toenails from the pressure if your laces weren't tight enough. That freaked me out so I tightened mine as best I could with cold sweaty fingers and then just went for it. When I hit the last part that was the steepest down, I was met with frozen chunks falling from the sky. "Really? Are you seriously going to hail on me?" I decided it was better than rain because it didn't stick to you like a drop of rain would.

I was never so happy to sit my butt down on that porcelain throne after hours of walking. I had purchased a standup female peeing device but decided to test my bladder's strength instead. My first attempt at using the lavender colored rubber sieve looking thing had luckily been in the shower as I peed all over myself!

The throne paled in comparison to the shower. I was surrounded by warm droplets of acceptance from heaven falling all over my cold, dusty, sore body. Carrying everything I needed on my back and walking up and down mountains put everything into perspective. I realized how many things I could do in not only a day but an hour. When I looked back and witnessed how far I had taken myself and my pack, it was an incredible sense of achievement. The things I used to take for granted I was not only appreciative of but thrilled about. That feeling stayed with me. As I walked from small town to small town, over freeways, up yellow hills and unmarked passages, I was always grateful for the bedrooms and the bathrooms.

A couple of days later, my fatigued feet walked into Pamplona barely taking the rest of me and my pack with them. The day had been filled with fields of wild flowers, smiling strangers and intermittent sips from my water reservoir. My shoes had sloshed through mud, water and grass. They had gone up and down and up and down stone paths, asphalt overpasses and this was only the beginning of my pilgrimage. As I entered the city over a beautiful stone bridge my obsession for picture taking was the only thing that outweighed my exhaustion. After many selfies and some poses taken by kind strangers I headed to the hotel. Yes, after the hellish night at the refugio the first night on the Camino I decided that I was not staying in hostels. I loved having my own room, bed and a shower I didn't need a token for five minutes of trickling tepid water that came nowhere close to bathing or soothing my curvaceous body.

I walked over 12 miles every day with these bones, muscles and fat. Yep, I'll admit it: on those days even my fat was tired. On one particular day, I had already walked 15 miles but I was desperate for clean clothes. There were certain cities along The Camino that had more access to laundry and Pamplona being a big city, was one of them. If it didn't happen that night it was going to be a few days. It was seriously the last thing I wanted to do but I changed into my back up outfit and walked my not so happy but determined ass another mile to the launderia. I wasn't there long as I only had 3 outfits. I was gleeful to have really clean socks and underwear that weren't just washed in a sink with cold water and paper thin soap strips from the outdoor store. I then returned to my room and started to get ready to go out again for dinner. I sat down on my gaudy floral twin sized comforter and when I looked down (to my horror) my ankles were the size of ripe oranges. My feet were also swollen and were hard to get out of my shoes. I wasn't in any pain and I guess that's why I didn't notice before. When I took off my hiking shoes to put on my nighttime aka recovery shoes, I could barely get the Velcro strap over the top of my foot. On the edge of my bed and sanity, I started to cry. Why was I doing this to myself? What was I trying to learn or prove? Normal people didn't do these things, what was wrong with me? Seeing my body deformed did something to me emotionally. My spirit for this pilgrimage began to damper. Luckily, Matt told me about a cream which saved my sanity and my feet. I don't know if it was cocaine or what that was in that cream, but the next day the swelling was half way gone. The other saving grace of that night was that I ate the most taste bud temptressing tapas I had in all of Spain. The damper was lifted and my thirst for the quest recouped.

I began to secretly gain the knowing that I didn't need to depend on a significant other to take care of me. Yes, I had been living on my own for over two years but this was different. It was my first time so far away from where I was born and raised, in a country that I didn't speak the language and I had to depend on only myself and the kindness of friends and strangers.

5

The Catalyst

Have you ever had your worst fear happen and then realize it was the best thing that has ever happened to you? Well, the worst and in hindsight, one of the best night of my life was Friday, March 9, 2012. I was sitting next to my wife and partner of almost 14 years on our suede chocolate brown sectional, three cocktails in. After months of conversations of her giving me percentages like, "I think there's a 40% chance we'll make it," I off handedly said," It's not like you cheated on me." Her response, was slow and a little slurred, "Well, actually…" and instantly I knew all of it. The other woman's face sizzling in my brain, her flames of hair against her pale skin and clear eyes. In that moment I knew why there had been so much distance, anger, and pain the last nine months. My life has never been the same since and I am beyond grateful every day. When a spouse is unfaithful and lying to your face every day and night, you know that there is something wrong, but you can't believe it, it is too painful so you blame yourself. I knew she would never cheat on me, she had the most integrity of anyone I had ever not just cared about, but known. I knew why I had felt like a crazy person and gotten myself to a therapist weekly. My entire fourteen years with my wife dissolved over those two words that took her less than two seconds to say. I had never felt the feelings that were forcing the screaming words out of my mouth at her. I couldn't even cry.

I had let her treat me like I was an irritating puppy that keeps jumping at your feet that you just want to go away and you pretend to kick it but wouldn't really do it. I had become so wrapped up in what would make her happy. I vanished.

The previous September I had started insemination for us to try and have a baby. I looked to her for everything. What I received in return were snide remarks and comments like, "Oh, I am not going to deal with this for nine months." So, after months of feeling like needy garbage I had reached my limit when she was finally honest with me about her affair.

I don't think she was expecting my reaction, I was DONE. The only reason I didn't leave the house that night was because I was too drunk. The biggest nail in the coffin that had been our marriage was the next morning. After a night filled with her visiting me in the guest room with tears and promises, I told her I would not be there if she left. Jay had promised the other woman to give her a ride to the volunteer function they were both supposed to attend. The woman's husband had their car and Jay felt obligated. I reiterated that if she left it sent the message to me that she was choosing her over me. She left. When the front door shut I knew all I needed to know: my marriage was over and I had no idea where I'd go or what I would do. What I was sure of: whatever I did, no matter how scary, it would have to feel better than being in that house and in that life with her. In my adrenaline haze and fury, I sent an e-mail to my friend who wasn't even in the country. I knew she had a studio behind her home that was unoccupied and thought maybe I could stay there. I also thought maybe I could go to where she was in Mexico. All I knew was that the last night I spent in my guestroom would be it. I would no longer live in the house we bought together less than a year earlier.

That night I had a girls' night with my gay best friend and sperm donor. I asked him if I could turn it into a slumber party and he agreed. He said I just had to bring my own bedding. In exchange, he plied me with lots of alcohol and my first Xanax. After that Saturday night I stayed at another friend's house for two nights, and then moved into the studio. I didn't know how much rent or utilities or anything was and I had no energy to care. All I knew was that I was free.

Even when circumstances surrounding you feel like you are in complete darkness, there is something inside of you that can propel you to the one twinkle of bright in the distance. My anger was what launched me. I could pretend that it was some higher consciousness or deep belief in myself but in those early days and weeks, the only thing I allowed myself to feel was rage. The morning I left her, I made sure that I kept my promise and was gone when she returned. I did not skulk out. I drove to Kohl's and bought a new suitcase. The other woman, (who I referred to as, The Whore) had borrowed ours and I most certainly would not be using it again. After purchasing the grey and black luggage on our credit card, I came back and shoved as many of my things as I could in them. With hot tears I said goodbye to our dog and closed the front door. Before I backed my black mini cooper out of that driveway, I made sure to gather up all of my lingerie and the ovulating and pregnancy tests that I had been a slave to the last several months. I stacked them intertwined in the outside garbage so it was overflowing. I wanted anyone that walked by to see the combination of black lace and bright pink sticks. I was no longer concerned about keeping up with the Jones'.

I had decided that along with the luggage set, I needed towels, sheets and other bedding. I could not imagine using anything from my old house. Besides the bedding, I felt I deserved some pampering. I went to a spa and got the works.

Upon opening the credit card statement and noticing all the charges, Jay texted me. The text said that I needed to curb my spending. Sitting in my new studio at my kitchen/dining room/only table, with a giant maniacal smile on my face, my fingers began to type something like this: "Take all of the money you spent on and with that whore, times it by 10 and then let me know how much more I can spend." Needless to say I never received that figure. In my best Hulk imitation, "Yea, you won't like me when I'm angry."

6

The Herstory of Us

I feel like you deserve an explanation, some background as to why I was so devastated when my marriage ended. More than half of all marriages end in divorce, so what's the big deal, right? It was a big deal to me because, well, it happened to me. We started out so connected, like a modern lesbian fairytale.

It was the spring of 1998 and Jay and I lived one building apart on the campus of the University of California, Santa Cruz. The first time I remember seeing her face she was auditioning to do a stand-up comedy routine for the Women's Ensemble Theater. I was one of the members deciding who would be in the show, and as soon as I saw her mischievous smile and deep sea eyes I knew she had to be part of the production. Her routine was on right before my spoken word/ dance piece. I remember getting so irritated that she made me laugh every night because she would switch up her act just enough to keep us all laughing. My performance was on something much less fun but I thought far more important to the lesbian feminist movement: At 22 I took myself and the world way too seriously.

A few weeks after the performances ended Jay asked me to

a production of Prometheus Unbound on campus. We then went to a party where I had jello shots for the first time. I proceeded to eat the fruit in the spiked punch, not realizing that's where a lot of the alcohol goes. We weren't driving, neither of us even owned a car. I actually didn't even know how to drive back then. So, we walked across campus through the woods and a few colleges, at least 30 minutes back to our prospective apartments. We came upon hers first and as we said goodnight we held our embrace longer than we ever had. As we pulled away I thought the sexual tension would actually keep us stuck together. She looked down into my longing amber eyes and said, "We probably shouldn't do this," and she bent down to kiss me. The full body charge in that instant felt like nothing I had ever experienced. Every piece of my flesh tingled with her touch. I was in my body and in outer space. I never wanted it to end. As the softness turned to more yearning my tingles turned into blazes. I had never wanted anyone as much as I wanted her at that moment. I have no idea how long that first kiss lasted but when it came to an end, the smartass in me couldn't help myself and I said, "What, oh is that what we shouldn't do?" We both smiled with sex in our eyes. I followed her into her apartment. We made our way into her single room, a luxury on campus. I had forgotten all about the fact that it was my time of the month and with the realization, became deflated that the sex would not be happening. I chose to be upfront about it because I had a feeling, in one place in particular that she was going to find out soon enough. When I told her she wasn't concerned at all. Her only words to me were, "I hope it's ok with you that you don't get much sleep because I'm going to have you up most of the night." Smooth, very smooth. That was one of the best nights of my life. It didn't matter that I was bleeding and we were on a single bed. Our bodies fit, like I was home.

That first summer we were together we lost so much weight, I swear all we did was have sex. I guess we slept, managed to work and when we came up for air, shared a delivered pizza because nothing else was open. I was living in San Francisco and she in Santa Cruz renting a room in a super religious Mexican woman's house. I would visit her on my days off after hours of public transportation adventures. She came to the house I was staying at but I lived with hoarders and we both didn't want to be there.

One night in her room, I asked her if she was thirsty. She said yes, I then replied, "Oh good! When you get yourself a glass of water will you get me one too?" We both laughed quietly because we were sure it was sometime in the middle of the night and didn't want to hear about how loud we were from the woman in Spanish the next morning.

One night, while Jay was living in the big yellow house we heard this mosquito buzzing for what felt like most of the night. We were exhausted after hours of sex, pizza eating and laughter. We had managed to fall asleep but then this buzzing would not stop. All of a sudden Jay jumped out of bed, turned on the light and grabbed her belt to try and squash whatever was making that sound. We looked at each other and started to laugh hysterically. We realized that anyone driving or walking by the busy street could see her naked ass standing, belt raised high, swatting at the air. How ridiculous a scene and how those types of moments endeared her to my being.

I moved back to Santa Cruz and lived with a roommate from the previous year. Jay got a room in a house that was with mostly queer women and it became the party house. We spent most nights together and began talking about marriage in the far off future. I had had a vision when we first started dating that we would end up together. I had gone to a candle making workshop and made two rainbow (of course!) candles and thought to myself, "These will be at our wedding," I shocked even myself because it was so early on, but I just knew. We never talked very seriously about marriage; it wasn't even legal then. I had mentioned that I was not a diamond person. I liked moonstones, and also emeralds. I felt marriage was fun to contemplate as I see myself as a romantic. I had no idea that Jay had saved her money and had a local jeweler design a ring for me.

The first summer we were together, broke and in love, we had walked from her house on Mission Street to West Cliff Drive to watch the sunset by a beautiful tree overlooking the ocean. Ever since then we called it our tree. One night, about a year after we started dating, she picked me up from work and asked if we could drive by it. I was hungry but said ok as long as we could make it quick. We got out of the car and walked around the tree on a beautiful June night. I wasn't paying much attention to her, breathing in the ocean air and resting my eyes on the sun setting over the horizon. She started talking and I could tell she was nervous. All of a sudden she was on one knee, an open ring box in her outstretched hand asking if I would give her the honor of spending my life with her. I had never been that pleasantly surprised in my life! I squealed yes! Both of our eyes teared as she put the oval shaped moonstone and white gold ring on my left ring finger. As soon as she placed it there, it felt right. We held each other in the love and magic of that moment.

A few minutes later my stomach started to growl. I blushed and we decided to leave and pick up dinner. We drove to Burger King's drive-thru, which might sound unromantic but we were just so excited. It might seem silly but Burger King still has a special place in my heart. When we got back to her room she had chilled a bottle of champagne in a silver bucket and there were a dozen lavender roses, my favorite flower.

We decided, okay, I decided, to have the wedding on May 27th because it was exactly one month after my birthday and a May wedding sounded fantastic. We were married May 27, 2000. It was not legal in California but we were so devoted to each other that we weren't about to wait for the state or the feds approval. Her co-workers at the time printed us a marriage certificate because they wanted us to have one even if the government didn't.

My wedding day was one of the most glorious. I owe most of that to Jay. She dealt with a couple of insensitive, self-absorbed bridesmaids. She also lined the aisle with lavender rose petals with her best friend. When we said our vows she was the one that cried. Our first dance was to our song, "Natural Woman," by Aretha Franklin. It represented how we felt and we thought the irony of us being lesbians was priceless.

We had many mornings where we would wake up and giggle at one another because we were so blissful. We would sneak home and do each other's chores so we could spend the weekend doing fun things like reading Harry Potter to each other, cooking or going out for a date night.

We called each other the love of our lifetimes. Before going to bed one night about eight years into our relationship she asked me, "Do I tell you I love you too much?" We told each other several times a day how we felt. It didn't feel like insecurity -more like sweet droplets of our love placed on one another. We were giant kids, too. She used to hide around the apartment or house as the years went by and frighten me. She always, always succeeded in scaring me. I had barely a C average at returning the favor. I was super competitive and would get grumpy which made her victories all the more magnificent to her and frustrating to me. One winter night in early 2001 I finally got an awesome scaring opportunity. We had an apartment with a long hallway she had to go down to get to the restroom or our bedroom. I decided to lie in wait for her. It felt like hours, but then I heard her size 10 ½ men's walk down the hall. It was finally my chance for scaring stardom. As I saw her toe turn the corner, bam! I tickled it. She jumped so high and screamed like a little girl. It was such a proud albeit immature moment of glory for me. Finally I had gotten her! She slid down the white wall onto the beige carpet next to me and we held each other as we rocked back and forth in our major case of the giggles. Years later we would recount that time and she admitted it was the best scare ever.

One of my favorite Christmases together I hand made her

a ceramic chess set. Both the king and queen were women. One side had tea items and cats, the other coffee and dogs. All of the pawns were gnomes with either yellow or blue pointed hats because those were her favorite colors; Jay had a fondness for garden gnomes. We exchanged gifts and as she was opening the chess set, I unwrapped an exquisite cherry wood jewelry box. I had no idea when I opened up all the drawers that there would be a ring box in the last one. In the soft white leather box was a delicate, shiny emerald and diamond ring. We were already married at this point and my moonstone and white sapphire wedding set was beautiful but not nearly as expensive as what I was staring at in this little box. I was stunned-- speechless for a moment: we didn't buy each other luxurious gifts. We lived in a studio above two single car garages. The gesture made me fall in love with her even more.

A few Christmases later, I attempted to make her pajamas which was hilarious, because I was no seamstress. Thank goodness I also made us giant stockings that made up for it! One year for my birthday she hand sewed a scarf out of a patterned burgundy velvet where she even added black fringe! She had asked someone to show her so she could make it for me. She always said I was the creative one and never made me things, so this was a big deal to me. I actually still have it. Our first Christmas together we painted clear glass bulbs for ornaments because we had very little money to decorate. Jay & I didn't care though, it was our first Christmas in our apartment as our own family.

Of course our relationship wasn't about the gifts we bought one another; it was the connection between us. We had our own language-- we could just look at one another and everything would be better. She was my knight in shining armor. She would stay up watching "The Deadliest Catch" waiting for me to go to bed while I drafted floorplans for an interior design school project.

I told her from the beginning that her blue eyes reminded me of the depths of an ocean. My eyes reminded her of sunflowers on a bright day. We would wake up in the morning and she would say, "Good morning my beautiful sunflowers." I would reply, "Good morning my ocean eyes." We'd giggled in bed for some reason or no reason, just because we were near one another.

For years it was like the best slumber party ever because sometimes there was sex involved. We would have died for one another. There were several years where I really did love every single thing about her. But then her oceans began to darken with pollution and my sunflowers turned away from the light toward sadness.

7

Becoming Blonde

Now that I've shared a bit of herstory, I hope the fragile state that my heart was in makes a bit more sense to you. After leaving my marriage, dog and house, I stayed with a wonderful friend who encouraged me to take some time off of work, call my therapist and pamper myself. I did all of those things. I was fortunate that my boss let me have three days off to try a regain something that resembled a life. My therapist was actually out of town and listened to me for at least thirty minutes straight while I incoherently sobbed and tried to tell her what happened. Having the embrace and safe haven of my friend's second bedroom I decided I did deserve to be pampered. I made an appointment to get a facial on St. Patrick's Day, exactly one week after leaving her. I loved to get facials, but did so maybe once a year as it was "frivolous" to Jay. I also treated myself to a manicure with a sultry red color and a matching pedicure. The woman who did my nails was such a hoot. I remember her big hair, loud laugh and that she just let me talk. She was a second therapist but she took smoke breaks, rubbed my hands and feet while making them pretty.

While I enjoyed all of the self-spoiling, the absolutely best thing I did was make an appointment with my hairstylist. He was surprised to see me on a weekday afternoon. Then, when I asked him what he thought about me being a blonde, he was not only surprised- he actually squealed! I think he was more excited than I was. He had been wanting to color my hair for years and secretly so had I. I didn't color my hair because Jay would say that I had the most beautiful hair color and why would I want change it? I don't know why I let her be that controlling. I convinced myself that I didn't want to color my hair because she thought it was so beautiful naturally and I wanted her to find me attractive. So: many years later with Barry, my hairstylist, just days after leaving her cruel behavior I was beyond ready to do this. Jay told me that she thought blonds were blah. I didn't do it 100% to spite her but that was the cherry on top for sure. I did it as a physical symbol to myself that I was taking back my life. I needed to be a different person, and the place, the only place, I had to start with was my appearance. I was at the salon for about two hours and when I looked in the mirror I was so pleased, I squealed too! I had not felt that beautiful in I don't know how long. To this day I adore my sunshine hair and occasionally being called Marilyn. With my new found confidence in being blond, I realize now how I opened up a part of myself that I had covered under many blankets, a giant crate and a padlock; that part of me was my sexuality. The blonde not only broke open that crate and threw off the covers but became a neon sign to single younger men(a few older) that I was very much available.

My sexuality was not the only thing budding at that time. My closeness with a few solid friends and my younger sister began to flourish. I counted on them to listen to my pain over and over. I reached out so that I was busy almost every night to either be comforted, listened to or distracted. I had no shame in asking for guidance and strength. The women I reached out to had been through love and loss in many ways. They helped me move out of my house. They gave me dishes, kitchen towels, chairs, etc. They gave things from their homes to help me make a new one. They held me and carried me when I could not move.

I remember calling my sister after I had moved in to my own studio. I wanted to shield her from what I was going through. Jay and I had raised her from the age 15-19 and even though I was devastated, I didn't want my sister to hate her. My sister, Persephone, was graduating from college and I knew I would feel responsible if she uninvited my ex. I tried to be nonchalant on the phone with Persephone about the fact that I was in my own studio. She wasn't falling for it and figured out time in her busy schedule of work and school in Southern California to visit me within 3 days.

I was surrounded by love. Not all of the love was even from humans. I call them my furry angels, or love pups, Mimi and Tili. From the day I moved in, they greeted me at the bay window wagging their whole butts barking excitedly whenever I came home. I'd wake up in the morning greeted with wet doggy tongues and cold noses; smiley, jumpy and exuberant to start the day. Unconditional love is magic, if only humans could do this with each other I believe we would not have wars. There is a kindness that washes over you when pure glee is looking at you through warm brown puppy eyes.

One love pup is part poodle and part jumping bean with curly white hair and eyes like an Egyptian queen with eyeliner and the longest white eyelashes I have ever seen! The other is longer, taller, black, tan and white. She's the one with the sweet puppy dog stare that melts your heart instantly espe-cially because she only lets a handful of people pet her. She has light brown spots above them that look like furry eyebrows.

The devotion of these dogs carried me through some of my darkest moments. That might sound crazy but if you have ever felt unloved and rejected you know how receiving any love is essential. Those dogs loved me every minute of every day no matter what cruel words I heard or awful memories flashed in my head; they were just there and all they wanted was for me to love them back. I well up with tears, even now thinking about how I believe they, a handful of friends and my sister saved my life. How do could I ever repay such grace?

I know that people don't love you for retribution. Rela-tionships are not about repaying kindnesses but about con-nections and sharing yourself. The depth of loyalty and sincerity I felt made me know that the joy I worked to obtain and feel was not only for myself. In my fragile first year, I clung to all of them in my sadness and anger. Their confidence in my hidden strength gave me what I needed to begin my self-excavation.

My fury became a close friend but I knew I couldn't de-pend on it for long. I turned to music to help me. I would blast "Stronger" as I sped up highway 1 whenever I had to see Jay. I would occasionally throw some Justin Timberlake, "What Goes Around Comes Around " in the mix as well, hoping karma would find her. After a couple months of this I began listening to less irate songs. I cherished my anger- it propelled me. I could not have changed my whole life through sadness or apathy. Anger and I were two peas in a hostile pod. I don't think I was ever an angry person per se, I was just so relieved to not be living in my old life. Between the anger and sadness was wild abandon. My ringtone for months was, "Wild One," by Flo Rida. My favorite line that I would sing to myself, "I'll show you another side of me, a side you never thought you would see."

The first night that I slept in my studio, I felt happier than any night I had spent in the ranch style 1985 house that I'd left with its 3 bedrooms, 2 bathrooms, and huge backyard for our tiny dog and our future kids. I was no longer lonely, sleeping next to someone in a California king bed. Instead, wildly sprawled out covered under my green double duvet. In the studio, I was able to be me. The studio became my cocoon/ sanctuary. It was surrounded by the lushest, most stunning flower garden with two quirky wonderful, loving dogs and two silly, cuddly (if I wasn't allergic) cats.

My anger taught me that I could be not only courageous, but fearless. If you don't ask, the answer is already a no, so why not ask? You could get a yes! When my whole life shattered in one moment, everything else didn't seem that scary anymore. It's not that I didn't have fear. The difference was when I thought about whatever the situation was, the consequences weren't as frightening as my marriage falling apart. Looking at it that way, in whatever situation it was, I went for it. In that way, the anger was easier.

But one Monday morning, my chestnut eyes opened a little gentler and my blonde head rested a bit heavier on my pillow. I couldn't feel my anger as strongly- I guess it forgot to it eat its Wheaties. Searching for what could be the cause of this, I scoured my onyx masterpiece-- the wall I built around my sadness, and discovered a miniscule crack. It had somehow appeared when I wasn't paying attention. How could this be? I had been meticulous in making sure it was impenetrable. That split could not be patched- instead it grew despite all of my efforts to stop it. That evening I understood that this fortress could not be repaired because it was now a gorge with grief waves rushing through it. I couldn't hold it any longer and it leaked out of my eyes as I shoved the orange chicken and broccoli beef into my face. I attempted to wash it down with 4 glasses of zinfandel and finally, quiet it with scoops of coffee ice cream.

A year later, at the doctor's office that grief had manifested to an additional 30 pounds on my body. I was trying to bury myself alive in order to not have to face the fact that I had lost the love of my lifetimes; we belived we had loved one another through several lifetimes. I realized it wasn't that other woman's fault. It wasn't Jay's fault or mine, it was no one's fault. If there's no one to blame, then what? Where could I begin to let the agony canal loose without drowning myself in it?

After countless months of countless tears, I was fed up with crying. I became exhausted with my own sadness. It was necessary of course to feel it, all of it, especially the feelings I most certainly didn't want to feel. Those are the worst and best of us all. When you unwrap the bandages that are holding your broken heart together and reveal the throbbing, self-loathing pieces of madness, you start to heal. When you can look at it in front of you and love it, like nothing you've ever loved before, your love invisibly stiches the pieces together. You find you have made yourself whole again. You are the only one that can do it. You are wiser, stronger, more confident and self-reliant. When you are whole again, please say yes, say yes to the adventure that is falling, being in and sustaining love all over again. Say Yes over and over and especially to yourself because that, my friend, is freedom.

8

Letting Go

My life was getting more and more awesome, so why did I miss Jay? No: I missed the idea of her. I missed what I had envisioned how I would spend the rest of my life. I missed the night where she asked me if she told me she loved me too much. The holidays made me nostalgic. I missed getting out all of our Christmas decorations and the year that I made us humongous stockings. I missed the egg nog sipping while we sang along to Bing Crosby's, "White Christmas" cd or John Denver and the Muppets. We would leave out cookies for Santa and would take turns sneaking out into the living room to leave each other gifts. We would wake up early, ok I would wake up early with excitement and make coffee and hot coco as we opened our gifts.

When my sister came to live with us when she was 15, we did the same things with her, I made her a stocking and we would wake her up with hot coco. I know she humored us in our gifts from Santa, Mrs. Claus, the reindeer and the elves, that was a tradition from Jay's mom that I loved. We would decorate the tree, Jay would put the lights up first and I would help her put the ones up around the outside of our apartment and be nervous whenever she got on the ladder. As far as the tree we had our favorite ornaments that we had bought for one another and gotten from family and friends, and after it was all done, we would turn out all the lights and sit, holding hands taking in the beauty.

Thinking about the wonderful times I spent with Jay drew me back to her arms, in all honesty a few times. The first time was only a few months after we had separated and I fooled myself into believing I could let all the pain go and we could start again. I had made a vow, a promise to love her my entire live and I don't break my promises. We both tried, but we were broken as a couple and it would not work, I hadn't forgiven her or myself for the pain we caused each other.

I would miss her and find myself back at the house in her bed. I can't explain why. Her love was familiar and comforting. Each time I knew it wouldn't last and finally we had a blow up. One night she continually called me and when I didn't pick up left a message, "I can always come over there if you don't answer my call." That was the only time I was frightened of her. Luckily, it was an empty threat and she didn't come over. I refused to see her after that and she retaliated by saying that I couldn't see our dog unless I picked him up when she was there. That was also after, "I don't even know what kind of people you're hanging out with now, maybe I don't want my dog around them."

I informed her I would not see her and if that meant not seeing Huck, then that was the choice I had to make; one of the hardest I made. My safety and happiness were the most important thing to me. I cried myself to sleep, sending my dog love and blessings that he would forgive me and know that I loved him.

Mediation

That decision led to months of Jay and I not speaking. I had served her with divorce papers and the court date was approaching. Jay wanted nothing to do with getting divorced and would not agree to mediation until I told her how much lawyers would cost.

Separated by the rectangular wooden table, what I used to call my "ocean eyes" that greeted me with love each morning had turned into iced over rivers of disdain. She barely looked at me but when I managed to catch her gaze, I felt those freezing waters send goosebumps up my arms. "We weren't legally married," the harsh words spewed out of those lips that used to kiss my body so gently. I held my breath. I couldn't believe she was using the bigotry of the state and federal government to deny our 12 years of marriage. What had happened to her? Who was this woman fuming across from me? It took me a minute to gather myself. I would not allow her to see the effect of her latest verbal puncture. My only comeback, "You're right we weren't legally married in the year 2000 but our domestic partnership was legally sanctioned by the state of California in 2003. I guess we'll go with that date as it is further back then when we got married the first day we legally could in Santa Cruz in June of 2008." I added that last part as a jab to remind her of all the efforts we had made through the years to prove our love. I would not sit there and let her reduce our relationship to nothing because she had become vindictive after I put the idea of alimony on the table. She was appalled that I had dared to ask for money from her. She honestly believed that because she earned more and that I left her, she should keep it all. She still lived in our fully furnished 3 bedroom 2 bath house with all of our belongings including our dog. Yes, I did choose to leave, how I could stay in a place that was a beacon of the lie that had become our life, surrounded by things that represented a life that was gone? I combatted her accusation of, "You're the one that left," with, "Oh and why is it that I left?" Embarrassed and a coward, I knew she wouldn't answer. She never admitted any wrong doing, and wondered so many times why couldn't we work things out. We sat there suffering separately in silence, scalding each other in the depths of our divorce as the mediator tried to move us through it.

Those meetings were so gut wrenching, after the second one I asked the mediator if I could meet with him separately, I didn't know how much more I could take. We would have died for each other and now she wanted to erase it all. Like it didn't count so she could reap all of the benefits of the last 14 years, claim to be the victim and blame me for everything. A nicely decorated package she could keep wrapped up for her convenience. I had other plans. I found my voice and to her surprise began to use it. My only question to myself was why I hadn't done so sooner.

The mediator informed me that I had to meet with her one more time. I had no idea how I was going to be around all of that emanating negativity. I would protect myself in my nice clothes with my hair styled and make-up flawless. I would blast Katy Perry's, "Part of Me," the whole way to the office and turn up the part where she sings, "In fact you can keep everything, yeah yeah, except for me!" I promised myself that I could yell, cry, throw things, eat a tub of Baskin Robbins jamoca ice cream, anything I wanted as long as I remained calm and did not take whatever bait she would put out there. I knew she would. I kept saying to myself that I was doing this for myself, she had the house, and what would I have? I deserved a nest egg, too, after all I had put my whole self into that marriage, including all of my earnings.

As I arrived at the mediator's office I said to myself, "I can do this, I can do this, and I can do this." I walked in wearing my knee high black boots, burgundy skirt, tight sweater with my leather jacket and deep crimson lipstick ready to take her on. For some reason she didn't feel as big to me anymore. Sitting there briefcase in her lap, obviously nervous, still angry but I couldn't feel it from the door. I couldn't believe it when it dawned on me, she didn't intimidate me anymore.

It took another long and torturous 6 months to agree on terms. After that we met one last time at the mediator's office and as soon as I got in my car tears cascaded down my cheeks. This part was finally over, we were officially over. It was a combination of relief, exhaustion and grief. I didn't want to be with her, it was just the finality of it all.

I tried to turn my heart off to her but I wasn't able to. I forgave her for the hurtful, awful, unkind, unloving things she said and did. I did not forget. I didn't dwell, I moved forward but she would not ever be the great love she once was, and that is what I mourned. I realized I can have two loves of my lifetimes or even three. I just needed to love myself wholly first.

Being in love in my early twenties, getting married, I fell apart when it didn't work out. I stopped believing in the idea that life would go smooth and happily ever. I believed in the ups and downs, compromise, giving and getting but not in total submergence with the other person. You have to be your own greatest love. I take myself to the movies, out to eat and even buy flowers for myself. Why not? Why do we only feel worthy if someone else thinks so?

Our Slow Demise

During that part in my healing process, I thought about how my relationship unraveled. How did we get to an affair, a mediator's office and rest of the mess? I think it began to disintegrate when I finished design school, my sister that we were raising graduated high school, moved out and Jay started graduate school. The house was empty when I came home from work. After years of celebrating Halloween together, (one of my favorite holidays) the October of 2010 I went to the pumpkin patch by myself. I think Jay carved one just to humor me. The next year she threw a fit and wouldn't even buy pumpkins or dress up. That Halloween we lay on the sofa in the living room of our newly purchased home, and in between trick or treaters held each other in sadness. In silence on the chocolate chaise sectional, arms and legs intertwined, we were lost in the knowing that we weren't in love any longer but couldn't fathom how we could live with or without one another. Six months earlier she had gone away on a business trip and was devastated to be away from me. I don't think we had slept apart since getting married. She had been at her father's and was so excited and nervous to pick me up at the airport. He had made fun of her and said it was only two nights, what was wrong with her.

I don't know if this is true for her but I think that changed her, I think being that lonely without me, freaked her out. I don't think it was healthy to miss each other so much that we were on the phone for hours before we both fell asleep from exhaustion but I think how she chose to deal with it was actually not dealing with it and running away from it.

As we lived through the years, we weren't in our twenties with few responsibilities. We had to grow up, pay more expensive bills and decide on what to do with our lives. The growing up part she took much more seriously than I did. Her seriousness then turned into nitpicking and controlling behavior. There were little signs at first; that's how it starts. She didn't like me going out late with friends and one night implied all of us were whores. When I called her on it she said that's not what she said. She was correct, she didn't actually call us whores. Jay was very good at inferring things and I let her. I slowly stopped staying out late or having alone time with friends. I began asking her what I should wear. Years into our marriage it got so bad that I just stopped asking because it would end up in a fight. Piece by piece I stopped being myself and turned myself into someone I thought she wanted and approved of. I so desperately wanted to be loved and wanted by her. I stopped wearing dresses and skirts except on rare occasions because whenever I did she would say things like, "Why do you always have to dress up? Why do you want me to look bad? You know I don't have anything like that to wear!"

After coming home all excited from getting my hair done,

I was crushed when she commented, "You look like my grandmother with that hideous fake red hair." Needless to say, I never had the audacity to color it again. I lost myself gradually, one outfit, one comment, one breath, one squinted eye glare at a time until I didn't know who I was. I became a woman that was there only for her wife. I only wanted her to be happy. I wanted so badly to be wanted, adored and loved by her and saw nothing else. Our sex life declined; it wasn't very vibrant after the first year anyways. I accepted all of it because I had convinced myself, with her assistance, that there was nothing else.

The last year of our marriage I don't even know who I had let myself become. She wanted to buy a house and I wanted to have a baby. We ended up buying the house first, then rescued a puppy and then I attempted to get pregnant. I had become the opposite of who I was when I had met and fallen in love with her. I put her in charge of my happiness, became so needy and sad. This was most apparent when I started the insemination process. Her reaction instead of comfort was disgust. "Oh, we are not going to have nine months of this," was her response when I asked her to change the five gallon water jug because I didn't know if I was pregnant and was worried about lifting.

Jay had tried to get pregnant years previously but then my sister came to live with us and we decided to raise her from when she was 15-18. The times that we did try it was very sweet and romantic. I would not drink alcohol or caffeine because she shouldn't. Years later when it was my turn, not only did she drink, she would go out without me to do it. Looking back that behavior was super codependent but I couldn't see it when I was in it. We became more and more codependent; not doing things without one another, everything together. I believe that those grains of sand started filling the hour glass of our demise.

After the attempts at insemination I never knew who I was coming home to. Jay's moods would switch, and if I was late or early I would hear about it. I lived under a constant strain of fear that I mistook as security. I decided to see a therapist and Jay objected to that; even though she had started seeing one. She said that I would see this therapist and then leave me. She had a way of saying things that when I let them seep into my spirit I felt so small and unworthy. Underneath the layers of obedience I found the courage to disobey her. I started seeing a therapist and when things finally blew up, I did leave her. She had made a self-fulfilling prophecy.

One Saturday morning on a neighborhood walk with my Pomeranian/terrier rescue puppy we stumbled upon the most vibrant dahlia garden. The flowers were behind a tall, dark wood fence which Huck sniffed wildly underneath. I spent several minutes peering through and over the fence, breathing in the orange, magenta and purple beauties. Huck and I meandered home and I looked forward to telling Jay about our find in hopes she would want to join us next time. My light heartedness instantly disappeared once I stepped over the threshold of my front door. The thick tension and pressure of not knowing what would be wrong had become a daily repression that seeped into my pores. I felt it as soon as I walked in the house. I headed quietly toward the refrigerator to get out breakfast stuff when Jay practically ran past me, "What took you so long? I told you I wanted to go for a bike ride!" My thoughts of the dahlias quickly scurried away with fright and I began my usual apologies, "I'm sorry, I didn't think there was a time limit. I just thought you were going some-time this morning. I'm sorry, I don't want to hold you up. Is there still time to have breakfast?" With a scathing look down at me, "Well not now, you're too late, God, I can't believe how inconsiderate you are!" She pushed by me on her way to get her bike from the garage. She put her helmet on and didn't give me a kiss or a glance as she left out the front door.

She began taking bike rides most Saturday mornings for months. She was trying to get in better shape and I supported that. I didn't understand why she was always so stressed about time and that it had to be around 10am. Jay could have left whenever she wanted but her reason to wait for me to be done walking the dog was that she didn't want to have to carry her keys and didn't want to leave the door unlocked. It never felt right but I went along with it because I didn't want it to be one more thing for her to scold me for.

The following March, I was at a stop light and saw a man riding a bicycle. I looked at him and a wave of realization broke all over and through me. My heart began to race as I un-covered what my wife was really doing when she was "going for a bike ride." Staring at this totally innocent biker, I knew why she had to be gone at 10am on Saturdays; that's when this woman's husband must have taken their two children out of the house. This bicyclist was the representation of my wife's affair. The waves just kept crashing, the bike ride was the perfect cover. She would leave to go have sex with this woman and then claim to be all hot and sweaty from the ride. I'm sure she was hot and sweaty form her ride all right. Ugh…too many images, noises and thoughts rushed through my mind. This was a puzzle I didn't want to put together. I sat there as the red light turned to green filled with this knowing. I didn't want to know this, I did not want to know this. I specifically told her I did not want to know any details and now here they were, flooding my mind and more painfully my heart. Now I know he was there, a band aid ripped off, in order to let yet another wound be exposed to breathe and eventually heal.

After I left Jay, it was the mundane things, like the bicyclist that would come up daily. I would be minding my own business and Wham! A smack right to my soul. It could be a light-handed one, like the smell of coffee or seeing her favorite color yellow. It could also be the heavy-handed smack of hearing "Natural Woman," our song, come on the radio at work. The secret sayings we would both utter; our twin language that I would hear her as I tried to shampoo my hair or brush my teeth. The tasks I took for granted that I would have given anything to just do on my own, without her voice, without her face, without her. I used all new products, ate at all new restaurants and didn't even watch the TV shows or movies we had watched together. I needed her out. But, it wasn't that easy. I ultimately came to the conclusion that the answer wasn't less of her, it was more of me.

At the end of December 2013, I was reading Eckhart Tolle's, "The Power of Now." There was a passage where someone asked how you get rid of negativity. His answer was that you just drop it. You drop the negativity as if it were scorching your hand. In that moment, I knew I had to let it all go. Something about that idea of not just releasing it but of dropping it like a pewter anvil just clicked and made sense to me. Holding on to it all was devouring me and so I dropped it right there. Since then, I have picked a little of it back up now and again but it mostly has been dropped and left there.

I had to let Jay know that I had forgiven her and myself. It was late on January 1, 2014 but I sent her an e-mail wishing her a year that was filled with much more harmony. I was honest about how hard the previous year was and that I hoped we could settle our divorce and maybe one day be friends. I sent it at 11:59pm and had no expectation. She and I were not getting along at all and I just spoke from my heart. Five days later I received an e-mail from her and it was better than I expected. I balled my eyes out reading it. She wished me joy and love in my life and told me that the years with me were some of the best of her life. She thanked me for sharing them with her. It was so emotional and incredibly healing to receive such a gift.

A Final Letting Go

Our mutual emails of kindness and respect were fleeting. After several dinners and attempts at a friendship, I realized my ex-wife and I were not meant to be in one another's lives. I should have cut ties with her at our first meeting after our divorce was final.

We met for dinner and the first words out of her mouth while giving me a hug, "What have you done to yourself?" As she looked down, literally and figuratively, at the new tattoo on my right upper arm. She then asked if I'd be joining a biker gang anytime soon. My response, "Not this year, maybe next." I wished I had been in a place of emotional strength and responded instead with, "What have I done to myself? I've become an even more beautiful, intelligent and amazing bad ass. Too bad for you that you'll never know." Then turned around and walked away, never to grace her with my presence again. Ah well, that was not the case.

Sadly, I stuck around for much more of her verbal and emotional abuse, as her, "friend." I slowly began to realize that she was an alcoholic narcissist. She had no interest in most of the things I had going on in my life or who I was, because they had nothing to do with her.

She spoke most of the time about her family that didn't talk to me anymore, our dog that I didn't see, our house that she still lived in and her work that was more important than our marriage. If she wasn't talking about those things she'd talk about new friends and all the things that she did currently that I had wanted to do with her, which she would never do.

By the time I gave up on the idea of being friends with her out of respect for our years together, I had a cacophony of grievances. It boiled down to this: No one else in my life was deliberately destructive and cruel. I had allowed her to treat me so poorly because it was our unhealthy dynamic and I was accustomed to it. But then one day, I was finally done. I had learned to love myself so much more than I had ever loved her.

9

Dr. Goosebumps

Less than one month after leaving my marriage, on Friday the 13th of April, I drove in the rain to Santa Rosa from Santa Cruz. While on 101 North I witnessed the most brilliant colors arched above the dark gray morning sky. Thoughts of raspberries, mangoes and kiwis popped into my head as I drove under its beauty. I knew it was no ordinary day; I had always seen Friday the 13th as good luck days. I was on my way to meet my occasional employers, a husband and wife team who designed dental offices. They had a new client and wanted me to meet him before we began designing his office. They would be showing him some examples of their work and wanted me to be there for the interior design perspective. I arrived shortly before he did; quite an accomplishment because I was usually at least 10 minutes late. They called him "Dr. Dean" and as he entered the building and noticed me I could have sworn his faint blue eyes livened a bit. He walked over to me and as he shook my hand, my entire arm, fingers to shoulder, tingled. I hadn't felt that way in YEARS. So many thoughts and emotions ran through my mind. What was that? Did he feel it too? Oh my, he was at least 10 if not 15 years older than me and he was a he!

After all the pleasantries, we piled in my bosses car and drove to the first office. The sexual tension between the doctor and I felt like it filled up every spare inch available in the 4 door sedan. By lunch our attraction felt like a neon sign flashing above our heads; please pay no attention to the fluorescent letters spelling, "We wish we were naked and alone together."

Dr. Dean opened my car door, touching my back as he held it for me while my fingers lingered over his hand on the top of the window. My perfumed body passed slowly in front of his spikey hair and flirty grin. He finagled a way to open the restaurant door for all of us, coming in right behind me, slightly brushing the top of my shoulders which ran a sexy shiver down my spine. He sat across from me at the table and as we looked at our menus, I felt his foot rub against my leg. My entire body flushed. What was happening to me?! I tried to focus on the menu. Someone asked what looked good and he stared right into my eyes and said, "I know what I want." I immediately looked away and thought how inappropriate and fantastic. I felt like asking, "Is it hot in here or is it just me?" I refrained and ordered my chicken salad.

At the last dental office, Dr. Dean stood very close to me. When I walked ahead of him he would lightly graze my upper back with his small but muscular hand. He was a dentist so I hoped he would be good with them. I then thought about those hands on other parts of my body and I realized I was not at all paying attention to the lobby or x-ray room. I only wanted to find a closet or a bathroom stall and jump on him. I had been a caged animal for years, finally set free around someone who obviously felt the same.

Back at my bosses office we all sat down at a large oval table where Dr. Dean proceeded to manipulate the conversation in a way to get my phone number; something about how he might want to discuss finish materials with me directly. "Finish materials," right! I'm sure that's what he wanted to discuss, but I didn't care. I wanted him to have my number, my address, my naked body at this point. He asked if I received his text but I hadn't. He tried again and this time it came through. It was only two words, "You're Amazing." Every cell in my body awoke and was set aflame. I wanted to leap over the table onto him and yet tried to act cool because my bosses were right there. Thrilled and slightly panicked to respond because I hadn't flirted with anyone but my wife in 14 years, I tried my best: "I think you're amazing, too." I coyly said, "I received your text, did you get mine?" We both smiled at each other and with a raised eyebrow he said, "Yes, thank you." Everyone was happy and made plans for getting the project underway. I was on Cloud 10 and then thought, how would this work? I decided I didn't care because I felt so alive. Words could not describe the high. After feeling so unwanted, not sexy or beautiful and unlovable, the idea of someone who just met me to say that I'm amazing, well, it did wonders for my self-esteem. I remembered what elation felt like.

Dr. Dean had to leave and as I shook his hand goodbye, I felt like a smitten teenager again. As soon as he left I skipped to the bathroom to text him that I wanted to see him. He immediately replied that he did too and how soon could we meet. My response was, "now," but he had to go home for his teenage son that was staying with him that weekend. We texted back and forth and he asked me to call him when I got back to my hotel room.

I was staying the night because I was meeting another client with my bosses the next morning. I made my way out of the bathroom and of course, they were super excited because he had signed their contract. They wanted to take me to a celebratory dinner (where I proceeded to use the bathroom twice because Dr. Dean keep texting me!); I told him I had to knock it off or they were going to think I had a bladder problem! We finished our delicious Mexican food dinner, and I was so anxious to go to my room to call this fantastic man, but they had other plans. They wanted to keep celebrating and go out for drinks. I, of course, had to say yes and be enthusiastic about it, but wanted nothing more than to call him.

After what felt like ten hours but was more like three, I finally heard his husky sweet voice on the other end of my cell phone. We talked for four hours and I basically vomited my whole sad tale on him. My separation so recent, it was all tremendously raw. I was an oozing heart wound desperate for sincere attention. He, I didn't realize at the time, was a gentle man willing to listen, comfort and show me how beautiful I was inside and out. He heard me with no judgement, just compliments and curiosity. He was also divorced but it had been several years. We talked about music, design, sex, you name it.

We then talked and texted every day until I went to see him. He lived four hours away and had his youngest son every other weekend. Our time was somewhat limited, but I didn't care. He told me that no matter what anyone, including him, said to me that I should never change the sweet and wonderful woman that I was. He also had a great way of looking at relationships. He said he wanted to wake up every day next to someone because he wanted to be there, not because he felt obligated. I had never thought about a relationship that way and instantly agreed 100%.

I drove up to see him on a Friday night. He took me to dinner at his favorite restaurant. He was so flattering. We just had fun laughing, talking, eating and drinking. Afterward, he took me to his office and showed me how it was and what he wanted the new design to be. We went back to his house or a better term would be his "villa." I thought I was in Tuscany when we pulled up. I was in awe, to say the least. The rest of the night was filled with mutually intense & beautiful pleasure. I felt so wanted and cared for. I wasn't in love with him but we enjoyed one another and it was perfect in that one night. The next morning we showered separately, got dressed and went out to breakfast. He had some business to take care of so I said I would leave from the restaurant. I would have stayed all weekend but I could tell he had other things planned.

We kept in contact but he dedicated his life to his son and rightly so. I had just left a marriage of over 13 years and was in no way ready for any type of relationship. He would text me random pictures of tomato plants or his trips to Arizona. It was a little odd, but I liked it. He even remembered my birthday the following year. His text message was very sweet, something about being the most beautiful person inside and out that he knew. I can't think of a better person to have had my first romantic involvement with in my new life.

Also, quite unexpected, I felt droplets of compassion sink into my heart for Jay. If she felt the way I felt with him when she was with that other woman, how could I be so angry with her? I hadn't felt fervor like that in years. I didn't even realize until he sparked it in me. I suppose that's what that woman did for her. It made me sad that we couldn't do that for each other but every piece of me knows now that I have to live with blazes not ash.

I know it sounds irrational but leaving my marriage was the best thing I have done, besides entering in to it. In some ways it's actually better because now I know myself and when we met I was a baby, barely 23 years old. I fell in to the "we" codependent trap instead of the healthy you and I coexistent. It's great to wake up in the morning and not depend on anyone to make you feel good. I've learned that of course you can feel adornment from other people but you are responsible for your feelings. The idea of security and "knowing," you will be with and depend on the same person for the rest of your life, was blown to pieces. I use the term, broken open, not broken to describe my heart, self and soul those first years. When your world is shattered you can fall with the broken pieces and crash to the ground or break free into the wind and soar into a new life that you create. I re-connected with the fire that I have always had inside me but had lowered the flames for another.

Looking back of course, she was not the only one to blame

for our slow demise and I know deep down in the places we don't like to go as humans, it had to be That bad, for me to leave my marriage. I would have stayed somewhat happy for the rest of my life. I chose the alternative, thriving in a new life I painstakingly molded with every tear, laugh, orgasm and taste bud. And even though my crush on Dr. Dean was fleeting, I knew I could date again.

10

Technology Free Weekend

I had decided to take a weekend off from my phone, social media, the internet and television. You might be thinking, well, what the hell did you do then? My answer: so many fun, relaxing, insightful and yummy things, you'll see! I had developed a minor addiction to my phone; especially when it was on and I had no plans with others. In those moments, I would look at it obsessively every few minutes, reemphasizing my tendency towards addictive behaviors. Instead of fixating on a text or something that I had posted on Facebook, I made myself sun tea from Lipton tea bags (I know, fancy). I took walks around my neighborhood, breathed in the salty sea air and most importantly spent time with just me.

I had begun reading self-help/spiritual books for guidance. I sat in my backyard on a black metal armless chair underneath a bright yellow umbrella and began to read Eckhart Tolle's, "A New Earth." Reading that book was the beginning of when I started trying to live in the Now. I thought being outside was the best place to attempt being in the Now, to see if this guy really knew what he was talking about. I cleared my mind, took in a thoughtful breath, released it slowly and focused on what I could see, smell, taste, touch, and hear. After only a few seconds, I felt how alive the garden was. I could hear the bees doing their jobs on the purple flowers; smell the scent of the white roses mixed with a hint of earth. When I deeply looked, there was this whole world of color surrounding me, from the intense blue cloudless sky to the brilliant magenta bougainvillea to the dulling grey concrete beneath my feet. I witnessed my own hands, knuckles, raised veins gently sloping through the top, my slender yet short fingers were tan; they had darkened from my normally very peachy due to the overachieving sun's rays.

What happened next is really what convinced me that this dude was on to something. I was reading about the pain body; where we store all of our pain and sadness that we have held onto throughout our lives. Thoughts of being a chubby little girl growing up in not-the-greatest neighborhood in Berkeley began to surface. I let the shame of weight, of wearing glasses before it was cool and the ultimate nightmare always being picked last (or on a glorious day, second to last) for a PE team just rise up and release through my wet eyes. I let the guilt go I had been holding onto about how happy I was when there was a fatter girl who was picked last and felt the shame instead of me. I told myself that I didn't need to take on her pain, mine was enough. I forgave myself for the shame I felt in the pleasure I experienced at her expense.

My mind then switched to my grandmother who helped raise me and would take me after school every day to Ortmen's ice cream parlor. It was on a corner a block from my elementary school and had a pink and white striped barber's pole outside. The stools were a bubble gum pink and even though I couldn't see over the counter I knew exactly what flavor I wanted. My Grams never judged my weight and just knew ice cream made me happy, so we went everyday she picked me up.

As I began thinking about my love for my grandmother, my tears began to lessen, and then all of a sudden I heard the music of an ice cream truck. I had lived in that neighborhood for over a year and had not once heard that sound and never heard it after that day. I was immediately taken back again to when I was a child and not only the parlor but the ice cream man who would come into the cul de sac of the apartments I lived in. A huge smile came to my lips. All excited I jumped up, put on my flip flops, grabbed my wallet and went in search of that melody. I passed the driveway, looked left and spotted the truck on the next block. There was a little boy with his father. For a second I felt a little foolish, a grown woman, 38, getting ice cream for herself. Then I thought, what is wrong with that? Who cares if people thought I was weird? I was weird and proud of it! I jogged down the street, not to miss my chance. When I arrived I didn't even know what to order and I just stood there, 7 years old again, in awe. I let my eyes feast on all the bright colors, cartoon characters that I vaguely knew, odd shapes, new and old flavors and bathed in the sweet glory of it all.

I can't remember what I ordered, it didn't matter. The importance was the knowing that there was something much larger than myself waiting for me to pay attention, and when I do, wondrous things happen.

Another example occurred that same summer. I decided

I would go to Spain and walk the Camino de Santiago the following April. I had no idea how I would afford it but I knew I would spend my 39th birthday on the Camino. At that time, I was living in a studio that was $1150 a month, about ½ of my income and completely essential because I needed my own space. It was my cocoon, my sanctuary where I could customize my own chrysalis and form my wings.

I didn't care that I was going into debt every month. I figured I'd be working at least 30 more years, I'd have it paid off by then. I had no idea how expensive the trip would be or how I would get 6 weeks off work. All I knew was that it was going to happen. Less than 2 weeks later the woman who was living in the main house with Ani, Gina was her name, announced she was pregnant and moving in with her boyfriend she had met 3 months earlier. Ani was freaked out about finding someone she could trust. I was like, "Hello, what about me??" Ani explained that I was her first choice but thought I wanted my own space and to travel without having the responsibility of pets. I said we could work it out; I just needed to have the time off the following end of April through May. Suddenly, I was able to afford everything to get ready for my trip and my trip! That's when I really started believing in (wo)manifesting and miracles!

11

In Search of Self-Esteem- Was it on a Stage or an Island?

After being with the same partner for 14 years, I needed to get re-acquainted with my sexuality. I thought I'd be brave and audition for a local burlesque troupe. I had performed in a dance group in high school, had done some belly dancing in my late twenties but nothing ever that daring. I also had a fondness, ok slight addiction, for wearing lingerie. I figured with burlesque I could combine two things I adored. A few weeks before the audition I bought some black booty shorts and a fake leather black halter corset, along with fishnets and stiletto heels.

The day finally arrived; a Sunday afternoon in October. I got dressed, onyx eyeliner and ruby lipstick added finishing touches. I threw a sundress over my outfit and proceeded to drive downtown Santa Cruz. I walked into the dance studio and immediately felt comfortable. There were 8-10 other women, all younger and thinner, along with two guys. I still felt very much at ease. The woman leading the troupe was a sexy slice of sunshine with a mischievous glimmer in her light eyes.

As I began dancing I had one of those moments; I call them "Observer" moments; where I watched myself dance almost naked in heels, rolling around on the hard dance floor. My knees and thighs hurt, my boobs were popping out of my corset, and my booty shorts were giving me a wedgie. I was trying the hardest to not laugh out loud at how funny this was. It was not a bad thing at all: The chubby, self-conscious little girl was now a proud curvy woman. I was embraced and completely out of place, an example of theory versus reality. After my comedy routine/audition, when everyone had finished, we sat in a big circle and talked about what our stage names would be. I had no intention of becoming a burlesque dancer anymore, but I chose the name "Sparkle." I imagined myself in sequins, rhinestones, glitter, you name it, covering every inch of my body as I performed. This was a fantasy that would remain just that because although I was captivated by the shoes, clothes, music and movement, being that intimate with strangers was too much emotionally for me. I was unable to be that exposed. I craved testing my own boundaries and making new ones. Even though I didn't make the troupe, I felt proud for showing up there in my new, sexy clothes, dancing my heart and boobs out and being able to appreciate it all. I decided that whoever is lucky enough to be my next long term partner, is going to witness quite a show!

First Holidays Solo - Yelapa

When the first holiday season loomed over me, I knew I could not be in Santa Cruz. I had shared 14 seasons of turkey and twinkle lights with my wife and knew I could not bear being in my home town. My life was upside down and I was floating somewhere outside of it. It was imperative to my already somewhat unstable mental well-being that I go somewhere, anywhere as long as she or our memories weren't surrounding my every view.

I decided to go to Yelapa, Mexico where my friend Ani, whom I lived with, had some property. This was going to be my first adventure outside of the United States by myself. Ani was meeting me in Puerto Vallarta but I had arranged my flight and all my travel details. Little did I know this would be the awakening of my slumbering traveler's soul. I had been the planner in my marriage. Somewhere along the twisting path of my marriage I began to believe that Jay needed to take care of me. This trip felt like the most important thing I had planned; I was proving to myself (unbeknownst to myself at that point) that I could not only plan a trip but live on my own and take care of every part of myself.

I arrived in Puerto Vallarta on the Saturday before Thanksgiving. Ani picked me up at the airport in a rundown old pickup that actually broke down. Luckily, after about 30 minutes we asked a nice man to help and he did. Another piece of luck, we were staying in Puerto Vallarta for 2 nights and the condo was not that far from the airport. The moment I stepped out onto the condo's veranda I let out the longest sigh; I overlooked water the color turquoise that's in the crayon box. The swaying palm trees reassured me that this was where I was supposed to be.

Later that night I woke up to fireworks. I could see them

perfectly from the balcony, all different colors and sizes, like large pom poms. Some kept exploding one inside the other, green, to blue then purple and pink; life exploding into beauty. I felt like the universe was celebrating my first holiday of freedom with me.

The next morning we took the water taxi to the island of Yelapa, the only way to get there, as there are no cars on Yelapa. This might seem an easy task but I was prone to sea-sickness and random bouts of anxiety. I was not excited about it, to say the least. I dug deep, pulled my big girl panties up, put on my anti- seasick arm bands and hoped for the best. The ride ended up being smooth, filled with a soothing breeze across my face, familiar Spanish words and genuine laughter.

We arrived about forty-five minutes later and basically had to jump into the water to get out, luggage and all. I had never done anything like that and knew this was going to be an adventure! Ani showed me to my palapa and it was the first time I had stayed anywhere without glass windows or wooden doors. The palapas were open air structures with no locks, made of some kind of thatch and wooden beams. I slept from a hanging bed that had mosquito netting and the first night I was paranoid at all the sounds, besides the waves crashing. I was convinced I was going to be eaten by some kind of jungle cat if I fell asleep. At some point I exhausted myself and felt that I had lived a good life. If a jaguar wanted to devour me they could, I just couldn't stay awake any longer. Fortunately, I woke up. It wasn't just any opening of my eyes; vibrant pink clouds and an orange sun like I had never beheld greeted me that morning.

At breakfast I admitted my silliness to Ani and I will never forget her response," You shouldn't worry too much, the jungle cats usually don't come down this far." In my head I was like, " WHAT?!?!?" She was not at all reassuring to my delusions of grandeur. She tried to help by saying I should be more concerned about the scorpions. Again, that was not soothing. But, I ended up having a wonderful week on the island.

That Tuesday, I walked to the main beach alone. I had lunch and a passionfruit cocktail that was almost the size of my head. I noticed people down the beach parasailing. I had watched them for a couple of hours until I decided to just go for it! I nervously walked over, shared smiles and signed who knows what kind of waiver; it was all in Spanish. I nervously put on the gear and started running as the boat took off in the water. Then, I was flying. Gliding over the brilliant blue water I was whoever I had wanted to be. Looking down, I say where I was staying, the coast line and little beaches in the cove. Music played in my mind, I was in paradise.

For Thanksgiving I craved doing something non-traditional. I figured a boat ride with strangers to snorkel and explore an island inhabited by the rare blue footed boobie was about right. After snorkeling and looking at the birds we arrived on an island where two gorgeous young Mexican men made fresh ceviche and carried it on their shoulders on a tray in the water from the boat to the land for us. They also brought us a cold beer to enjoy with it!

On Thanksgiving night I was so excited about not eating anything remotely like an American turkey dinner. But, how excited Ani was to tell me that we were going to the only restaurant with other Americans serving a traditional thanksgiving meal! Life, had a wicked sense of humor. At least I got to have margaritas with my turkey. Most importantly I had proven that I could enjoy a holiday without my ex.

12

A Fetish Site, Threesome and Man Sex, Oh My!

I spent many a year trying to figure out and define my sexuality. I am sexually attracted to masculinity, female masculinity. I was married to a woman, a woman who most people thought was a man. She dressed in only "men's" clothing but did not identify as transgendered. Before Jay I had dated both women and men. The first few years after leaving my marriage, I needed something easy and that would boost my self-esteem. That equated to younger men. I knew that Butch women were my passion but also my kryptonite. I had no capacity to really be in a relationship. This might sound harsh, but younger men only wanted to have sex and have fun. That was all I was capable of so, it worked out perfectly.

I was not only curious about being with new people but also different types of sex. The September after I left my marriage I wanted to explore the world of kink, fetishes and what the BDSM community was about. I had heard of the Folsom Street Fair but didn't know of anyone that would be interested in going. I was a little nervous going by myself but I decided to change into something I normally wouldn't wear in public during the day. I decided to wear what I wore to my burlesque audition and added some knee high boots. I was lucky enough to find a parking space within two blocks of the fair so I only had to wear my outfit in the general public for a couple of minutes. Once I was inside the fair, I felt so comfortable! The feeling I remember the most strongly was that I wished people could dress this way every day if that was what really made them happy(minus all the exposed penises). Everyone was free to express themselves with no judgment or ridicule. It felt so fantastic to walk down the street in broad daylight dressed the way I was and not be the most wild by far. I wasn't a freak that didn't belong, I was accepted. On that day in that space I got to glimpse a little inside the kink world and I liked most of what I saw.

That night I decided to check out a fetish site that I saw advertised at the fair. The whole dating thing was such a foreign concept to me. Even though I was 37 when I left my marriage and not old by any means, I just felt awkward in the dating scene, I hadn't dated in fourteen years. Trying to have confidence and not seem desperate or worse feel desperate, I had attempted the online thing before. I tried several sites and went off and on depending on my seriousness with it. If I took it too seriously it drove me crazy and plummeted my self-esteem.

I thought maybe the fetish site would be better or at least different. It was different all right! Let me tell you: that was some crazy, ultra-sexual, in your face, not for the faint of heart, kink! But, on the site it felt freeing to not feel alone in wanting to explore more than conventional sex. I ended up "friending" several people and they were all quite normal, not the stereotypical scary freak, one might assume was on "those" sights. I found they were just people that wanted to meet other people.

What I came to realize was that I love wearing corsets and bondage type gear but that I am not into the "life," I'm not interested in being anyone's master or slave. I don't want to physically hurt anyone or vice versa. When I find someone that I feel safe with I think it could be fun to tie them up and pleasure them and vice versa but nothing too serious. I'm interested in sex as an activity that lasts; lots of foreplay, spanking, maybe some chocolate dipped strawberries fed to me, the list goes on and on. I see sex as fun. It can be a quickie and very hard and fast intense or it can be long and drawn out and drive you crazy in anticipation for hours.

In my marriage, sex was an issue. I was the one who wanted to have more of it and it was a discussion for a while. I know there was obviously more than sex when you are invested in a life with someone. My excuse used to be that I was born in the year of the rabbit and am a Taurus that is ruled by the planet Venus – of course I wanted to have lots of sex! It's not that my ex didn't like sex. The first few months of our relationship we didn't get out of bed. As time passed we would have discussions and it was always that we had different needs. I turned my healthy sexual appetite into something that was wrong with me. I was dedicated to keeping the sexual relationship alive in my marriage and until the rejections became so frequent and hurtful I gave up. I think that was one of the reasons the affair was such a betrayal. I just really couldn't wrap my mind around it. That fueled my intense anger with her. Being confined with what we did in the bedroom and the scarcity caused me to just bust out when I left my marriage. I was ecstatic to have lots of sex again. I needed to prove to myself that my ex was the one with the issues, not me.

The last time I initiated sex in my marriage was when she told me to be quiet while being intimate. I was devastated. Shame overwhelmed me. The feelings of rejection and being unlovable took turns carving away at my self-esteem. It took many new sexual experiences for me to be able to not feel self-conscious or if I was "making too much noise." I began to realize that sex was fun. I don't apologize for loving sex anymore. I value sex, everything about it. I like having my body touched everywhere. Yes, it's nice to be caressed in a gentle way and with care but I think if someone is throwing you around your bed there is a connection there as well. We are animals and I'm not apologizing for loving sex anymore. As a woman I get all kinds of advice, you should not give it away on the first date, you should wait until at least the third date. My answer is maybe I won't want to have sex with them on the third date so why wait. "Men won't take you seriously or will think you're a slut if you sleep with them right away." I honestly don't care what they think. I believe in the Now and have no idea what will happen next week, tomorrow or in 10 seconds. If I'm attracted to someone why not enjoy. I think of sex as an activity like going to the movies but more interactive. A man I had sex with recently called it naked partying. I'm not suggesting that you or anyone else just have sex with random people all the time, unless that's what you'd like to do. I try to not give advice but when I do it is the same: follow your soul, don't apologize, be yourself.

Owning my sexuality has been one of my hardest struggles, from trying to define it to embracing it, to reveling in it. I sometimes think that cats have the right idea, they let you pet them and snuggle them and you kind of know when they're done but if you keep petting them they'll bite you. I think we humans would feel so much better about each other if we didn't lie and cheat and when we were done we just gave each other a gentle nibble and then left.

Unfortunate looking Kyle

The first younger man I met was Kyle. We met at a local bakery, someplace so benign, considering we met on the fetish website. We had also been exchanging the most sexual texts I had ever experienced. I can't really explain why it was so exciting except that my ego liked that he was 12 years younger, so complimentary and hilarious. He was not very attractive, I could just say he had a "great personality" and you'd know what I meant. I figured I'd be blunt.

Maybe because I hadn't had sex in a while, I was ovulating, I have no idea why I was hanging out with this man child because he was seriously unfortunate looking. Let me be clear, he was not disfigured in any way or suffering from a debilitating disease, I'm not that heartless, he just wasn't attractive to me. But, did that stop me from extending the date, not at all. After our conversation and cookie consumption we ended up getting a hot tub. What a bizarre first date, cookies, hot tub, sex and then an ice cream cone. I know this is horrible and I'm not sounding like a good person here but in all honesty, at the ice cream kiosk I kept looking around to make sure no one I knew was around. I had let him see me naked and do all kinds of things to my body but oh no, couldn't let anyone I know see us together. Note to self: if you are embarrassed by a person and don't want to be seen with them in public, don't date them and certainly don't fuck them.

Did I learn my lesson after that first encounter, of course not? I saw him one other time because I thought maybe I was being shallow and the sex was fun, so why not? I had him over to my place, of course I did; I didn't want anyone else to see him! So terrible I know, I really am a kind and compassionate human being I swear! So, I opened the door with this pink and black corset on and these fabulous black stiletto heels with feathers on top. I could barely walk in the heels but that wasn't the point. We moved right to my bed which wasn't far because I was living in a studio. We started messing around, got naked and started having sex. I figured at some point he would put on a condom. I don't know why I let him inside without one but I did and he never put one on and finished inside of me.

That was my lesson in how I needed to be in charge of my sexual health. I was furious at him and in hindsight more furious at myself. He apologized several times and said he'd never do it again. He was right about that because I never saw him again. My reason for sharing this most intimate and shame ridden experience is so you or someone you know that has been in that circumstance knows that you don't have to feel like an atrocious human being. We are people and we can let certain body parts overrule our better judgement. I am not trying to justify my behavior and I am a strong proponent of safer sex.

I have grown weary of women's self-shame when it comes to their sexuality and sexual escapades. I have learned from my slipups and have moved on. I also mention this because on that particular day I was ovulating. I went to the pharmacy to buy the morning after pill. You might think, no big deal, women do this all the time, but for me exactly one year prior I had been trying to get pregnant and was praying every day hoping that I was. A year prior, having a baby was my number one goal in life. The irony that I stood in line for a pill that would prevent the one thing I had wanted more than anything the previous year, was certainly not lost on me. Swallowing that white oval capsule I smiled as the sunlight hit my face in the tiny studio that had become my sanctuary. I lived somewhere I was free to be myself in all of my bumpy glory.

The Ménage

A little over a year of being single, I went downtown for my friend Saturn's birthday celebration at a local Irish Pub. I met new people and chatted with them and mutual friends. I immediately noticed a tall, broad shouldered man named Cam, with shoulder length dark curly hair and my weakness, blue eyes. I was drawn in and lucky enough to sit across from him so I could look into those blue beauties slyly, now and then. Sitting next to me on my left was this beautiful woman with long sandy blond hair, named TJ. She had full red lips and black eyeliner highlighting her striking oval eyes.

I am not usually attracted to feminine women and definitely not straight girls. I found out she was straight because she had been talking to me about this loser ex-boyfriend of hers. We were comparing notes about online dating, the pros and cons and insanity of it all. A group of 6 of us chatted, laughed, and drank more and more. A few of us didn't want the night to end because even though it was Sunday, the next day was Memorial Day. We walked Saturn back to her bicycle and everyone except myself, Cam and TJ went home. There was some teasing about who Cam should hook up with, me or TJ; all in good fun. Then someone yelled out, "I think a threesome," and we all laughed. The 4 of us walked to another local bar and once there Saturn decided she'd go home and leave the 3 of us to delight in getting to know one another more. We entered the bar and I found out that both Cam and TJ had an affinity for whiskey. I had never drank whiskey but thought, what the hell! We managed to score a sofa and TJ and I sat on either side of Cam. For some reason the whiskey shots were on special that night, I honestly don't remember how many shots I had, I think at least 5, maybe 6?? At one point Cam had his arms around both of us and a guy came up to him and said, "This is not fair, you have not only one hot girl, but two. You can only have one, one guy one girl, what about the rest of us?!" Cam just smiled. Fortunately, he lived right around the corner. TJ and I had decided at one point that we were going to crash at his place. We left the bar around 1am, details are a bit hazy. Instead of going right to his place we all thought it would be a fun idea to go to the neighborhood park. We played on the jungle gym, tried to figure out what, in our drunken stupors, the animals were supposed to be the metal structures that rock back and forth. I attempted to ride one and that attempt was futile. We had Cam push us on the swings and at one point we all laid down in the tanbark (which I don't recommend by the way, too many splinters.) and looked up at the stars. We thought we could make out the giant dipper and were trying to be astronomers totally drunk off our asses, lying next to each other at 2am in the totally uncomfortable tanbark.

At some point we went to Cam's place. Once there he gave us glasses of water and realized that his kitchen was fuchsia and he had a light pink refrigerator. Every room in his apartment was painted a different color, purple to green to yellow! It was a good conversation starter because I think we were all kind of nervous, drunk and tired. We also weren't sure what, is anything was about to happen.

We ended up all sleeping in our clothes on top of the bed horizontally across it, with TJ in the middle. At some point Cam moved to the middle. It was actually quite sweet; we all spooned each other and even though there was sexual energy in the air we all just held one another until the morning.

I must admit I was a little bummed at first, I really wanted something sexual to happen with all of us. I finally let go of the idea and fell asleep. Throughout the night we would exchange kisses and soft touches, but it was all fairly innocent and sleepy.

When we all woke up and Cam took a shower. He took quite a while and TJ and I thought we should either join him or leave. It was a little awkward and we were so hung over. Cam came out of the bathroom with a ratty blue towel wrapped around his waist and I can't remember how we all started making out but all of a sudden the three of us stood in a circle. My tongue was in TJ's mouth, my small hands grabbed her large breasts, while she was touching Cam's chest and he kissed my neck. We moved to the bed and I took TJ's shirt off in a flurry of excitement and nervousness. I then freed her breasts from her lavender lacy bra. I noticed her soft, then harder perfectly pink nipples. Cam took off her pants and she said, "What have I done to deserve this?" I replied, "Just being yourself," as I kissed her.

A moment later she said she was embarrassed by her underwear and that she would have worn sexier ones if she would have known. Cam and I didn't care because we all ended up naked. We all kissed and touched one another. Cam actually ended up doing most of the "work." We kept that boy busy! The whole thing was an incredibly sensual, open, honest encounter. Of course it was sexual too but it was beyond just the sex. I know that might sound odd since the three of us only met the night before but there was a sweet connection between us. Everyone felt included, fulfilled and a part of something that not everyone lets themselves experience.

I often wished we could have done it again but it wasn't in the cards. For a little while we both ended up dating Cam. He was up front with us both and didn't have sex with either of us until TJ told him she would like a relationship with him. I appreciated his company and my feelings were a little hurt but they made a much better couple. According to TJ they only slept together a few times and never got serious. We all still know each other and are friends on Facebook. When the three of us have seen each other there was a lovely flirty, sweet vibe, which I appreciated.

The day I had the threesome with TJ and Cam was not just Memorial Day. It was May 27th and it would have been my 12th wedding anniversary. There was a part of me that wanted my life with her back so badly, the person waiting for me when I got home, the familiar touches and glances; but the only thing remaining from that life were the tares I was still mending on my heart. There was no authentic rekindling that could happen or starting new and fresh. How can you do that with someone you've shared a life with for over a decade that was controlling, cheated on you and treated you like shit? Being in bed with two wonderful people I realized that a life of unknowns was the life I chose. I could have been with Jay in our house with our dog but instead I woke up with strangers and was euphoric to be there. Having a threesome with people that are not your wife on what would have been your anniversary pretty much summed up how I felt about my marriage, it was over for good.

The Lioness vs. the fresh meat

The day before my 38th birthday I was walking my dog (at that point I was still attempting to share custody of), while on my lunch break. My shared dog was intently smelling something and then decided to wait. In my head I said, "Thank you Huck!" because I was instantly distracted by a young man that was walking towards us. His rich caramel skin and tight muscled arms that seemed to glow from underneath his white t-shirt, made me catch my breath. He bent down to Huck and was talking very sweetly to him. When he stood up I noticed his chocolate pudding eyes and charcoal wavy hair. A dark wave fell ever so slightly to cover one of his eyes when he began to speak; I wondered if he had planned that. His lips were full and I had a hard time concentrating on what he was saying. Between his eyes, lips and the muscles popping out of his tight t shirt, good God, this man had walked out of someone's fantasy and thankfully into my reality.

He introduced himself as Henry and that he was staying in the neighborhood. We spoke briefly and I told him that I needed to get back to work. He asked for my phone number and I rarely gave out my number but I didn't have anything to take down his information so I threw caution to the wind and watched him enter the digits into his flip phone. Henry also seemed young and I hoped he was at least 25. I doubted he was even going to call me so what did it matter. When I heard my phone ding with a text message around 4:30 that afternoon, I figured it was my birthday buddy, Giuliana, about plans for that night.

Giuliana's birthday was the day before mine and we usually did something together with mutual friends. When I grabbed my phone from my purse I couldn't believe it was from Henry. His tagline after his texts was, carpe diem, which I felt to be perfect for this situation. I told him that I could call him later because I had birthday plans. When I arrived at my friend's house they had a great time teasing me about meeting a man literally on the street. I describe him to them and then they're only concern was, how old is this one? They knew about my fondness for men at least a decade younger and then I reassured them that he told me he was 33; I'd waive the age restriction due to his gorgeousness. We all had a laugh about that and I continued to secretly or not so secretly text him throughout the evening.

Later that night I called him and we talked for hours, he wanted me to come over, he was staying at the Hitch n' Rail motel around the corner while in the process of getting a place in Santa Cruz. I was tempted but the following day was my birthday and I was getting a tattoo colored in and throwing a dinner party for myself. I needed sleep and knew that would not happen if I saw him that night. He swore to me that he was very shy and would, "Probably just hide in the corner," when I got there. I told him I didn't believe that for a minute and I knew exactly why I was getting up at 7am to meet him.

I adored celebrating my birthday and woke up excited. What an amazing day ahead! I found my sexiest pair of black lace panties with matching bra. I had come to the conclusion when I left my marriage that life was too short for boring underwear. I put a pink dress on over the black laciness, had some coffee and drove around the corner promptly arriving at 7:30am.

The moment I knocked, he opened the door, and it slammed shut with the weight of our bodies. It was on. He wasn't wearing a shirt and neither was I after about 30 seconds. The sexual chemistry between us was like a lioness and a piece of meat. We took turns being both predator and prey. Everything about him was hard, his six pack abs, the way he thrust his tongue inside my mouth when we kissed, just the way he handled me.

My panties became a mess of wet fabric soon to be discarded on the carpet. I opened his jeans and took them off to expose his boxers. The energy was frenetic. We finished taking of each other's clothes, and he was sucking on my nipples while throwing me on the queen sized bed. Once on the bed he started licking my thighs and can I just say that man's tongue knew its way around a woman's body. After writhing in pleasure, I released his head from between my legs and he climbed up my body and put himself in my mouth. He had the largest cock I had ever experienced at that point in my life. Size is not a thing for me and I usually have a gag reflex but there was something about his confidence and sexuality that made me want to please him. I wanted his hardness all over me, inside me, everywhere. When he couldn't stand it any longer he came all over my mouth and face. He got a towel to wipe us both down, we were sweaty, sticky piles of human wantonness.

I think we rested for about 20 minutes in the over 4 hours of sex we had before he had to check out. It was a whirlwind of hot body parts crashing in to one another. He was my first and only experience with anal sex. I was hesitant at first but as I was in such an experimental place in my life, I tried it. It wasn't bad, he made everything sexy. I think the reach around while he was inside me is what made it the most pleasurable.

I know this is graphic and the most sexually explicit I have been, but Henry was the most sexual and intense person I had ever been with, at that point. I was able to explore pieces of myself I had been too ashamed to even think about, let alone act on. I am sharing this so explicitly because I believe women have the right to lust and pleasure. We owe it to ourselves to revel in every single second of sex, to own it and say, "Yes, I love fucking and being fucked!" It doesn't have to be all sweet, soft kisses and cuddles after. We are animals and when there are consenting adults, why not partake in some animalistic pleasures. I'll remove myself from my kinky soap box now. I wanted to explain the reason for my graphic depictions.

After leaving that motel I thanked myself for the best birthday present I had ever received, 4 hours of orgasms and sex with a rock hard 33 year old brown skinned god. A serious Happy Birthday to me!

That first time was off the charts. The second time was more of the same but everything about him was intense. It turns out there was the tiniest of twists to the story, as to why he was staying in motels. It turns out he was on parole. I know that you are thinking, but, I looked over his case and heard his side of the story. I believed him. Even though he was a beast in the bedroom he was a caring and thoughtful person. I felt a genuineness about him.

He told me stories of time spent with his nieces and nephews, his large Mexican American family and how close they all were. He was mostly obsessed with his court case; rightly so, he couldn't get a job, and it was a bit of a nightmare for him. I think he had PTSD from being in jail the previous eighteen months. At this point you might be thinking, huh? Really? You're involved with a recent parolee, how desperate are you? What, what, what the hell is wrong with you? Trust me, I asked myself those very same things, as did my concerned therapist. I can't describe it, the chemistry was insane between us. I was addicted to the passion. It was all fire, all the time with him. His strong arms that would hold me down as he talked dirty to me had me coming back for more over and over. We would be in one random hotel room for hours upon hours. That was all we would do. It was fantastic and exhausting.

After a month of this and the relationship always being about his case, his life, I couldn't handle it anymore. I was honest, and told him that he was a great man and amazing lover but it was all too much for me. I was still dealing with my break up and wouldn't take on anyone else's drama. Of course, we kept in contact and I mistakenly answered his phone call one night and ended up 20 minutes later at his latest hotel for another few rounds of what we had in common.

After seeing him a couple more times I told him that I had begun dating someone else, which was true. We were just dating, nothing serious but openness and honesty were incredibly important to me. Henry didn't want me to see anyone else so I told him that we were done. He understood and I didn't hear from him again for about a year. That phone call I declined, but damn that was some awesome sex!

13

The Horrors and Whoring of Online Dating

As part of the process of discovering aspects of my newly embraced love of my sexuality, I chose to date online. I hadn't been in the dating seen since being in my twenties and heard online was what people did. I don't even know where to begin here! Online dating was so many things; a few adjectives: bizarre, irritating, hilarious, ego-boosting and ego-thrashing. I relished it more than dreaded it, so I decided, why not put the energy into it? I was on different sites and then got off of them when I started taking the whole thing, mainly myself, too seriously. But, it sure made some titillating experiences and stories!

The Hair Model

The hair model was, as you can guess, eye candy with thick, dark wavy hair. He was Italian and Spanish with olive skin, earthy rich eyes and a muscular body to match. He lived in San Jose and it took him three sentences on Match.com to start talking about sex. He was so striking, I didn't care. I know that sounds super shallow and that's because it was!

At that time in my life I was in no shape to be involved in

anything that could even be called a relationship. My fondness for men in their late twenties was in full bloom. The sex without attachment was all I could manage, my heart was closed for business but my body flashed a neon OPEN sign as often as possible.

The hair model in our first conversation went on to tell me that with his ex they did it 10 times in one night. I eye rolled, "Yea right," but I played along. The next day while I was at work he kept texting me all these things he was going to do to me when we met. He was very imaginative and descriptive. It was also so inappropriate for me to look at while running the front of a dental office. Luckily, my co-workers were totally fine with it since I shared some of the details and managed to get my work done. They had a bet if I was going to meet with him and go home alone or with him. I told everyone that I, of course, was just going to meet him for a drink, knowing pretty much 99% that he was coming home with me. Unless I got a creepy vibe or our chemistry was only on the phone, he was so coming home with me.

After work that Friday, I talked to him on the phone about meeting. He couldn't talk long because, yes, he was in the middle of a photo shoot. I have to admit, he did have great hair. If his sexual skills were 1/10 as good as his hair, I would have seen him again. Harsh, I know but I think you'll agree with me when I'm done.

We met at a swanky bar downtown and when I arrived I noticed him right away. He was wearing a long sleeved, deep pink collared shirt, very expensive jeans, belt and leather loafers. He looked like a model but he was so Silicon Valley, not Santa Cruz, at all. He really was as gorgeous as his pictures so I thought why not have a drink and see where it goes. He was polite as we ordered our drinks and made small talk. I asked about his photo shoot, we talked about his daughter, my dogs, etc. We were done with our second drink and mutually decided to go back to my place.

On that night I had the house to myself. We arrived and I decided to show him the beautiful backyard. Ani created the most wonderful flower and vegetable gardens. So we were by the vegetable garden and started kissing. He was a good kisser but it went downhill from there. We started grabbing each other and taking off articles of clothing; he was passionate I'll give him that. After a few minutes we made our way inside to my bedroom and started having sex. We went at it for a few hours and I liked it, but not nearly as much as he did. He was so into himself it's actually kind of funny looking back on it. He had climaxed 2 or 3 times and when I hadn't I asked him if he would be so inclined to help me with that. Isn't that part of why we were both there? His reply, "I'm exhausted sweetheart, sorry." What a dick!

The next morning didn't even offer. I didn't offer either, I was over him. I had not experienced such a selfish lover before and thankfully I haven't since. We originally discussed spending the entire next day in throes of passion but at around 8am I waved goodbye to him.

I figured I wouldn't hear from him but that very night he called. I told him it wasn't going to work out and when he asked me why, I asked him if he really wanted me to be honest and he did, so I told him he was self-absorbed and a lousy lover because it. His defense, I should be excited that he climaxed 3 times! I should be excited for him, unbelievable!

He said he wanted to make it up to me. I told him if he was serious, he could drive over the hill and take me to dinner, just dinner, no sex and we could go from there. I'm sure you'll be shocked that he didn't take me up on my offer. Strangely though, about a month later while I was visiting my cousin, up on her rooftop patio around midnight, he sent me a text message asking if I had experienced any luscious cock lately. Needless to say I did not reply.

The Guitar Player

After my not so thrilling experience, I waited a few weeks and was back at the online thing. Feeling bored and not too optimistic, I scrolled down the countless male faces. A few clicks down, something snapped me out of my online fatigue. I had no idea that the lake blue eyes I landed on would belong to a 28 year old who would be the best first date I had ever had. The impish grin that spread half way across his face that implied naughtiness I might be able to experience with him, is what got me to message him. He answered me right away and actually wanted to talk to me on the phone. In the online dating world this can take weeks to get to. I liked his boldness. He didn't want to waste time messaging when we could speak and see if there was chemistry. After our first conversation where I found out his name was Phil and he delivered oxygen and other gases to dental offices and I worked at a dental office, it seemed like a good sign. Totally superficial, but I went with it and we made a plan to meet.

It was a warm Tuesday, late August evening and I got there

about five minutes before he did. I was able to witness him saunter out of his white work truck with a big ring of keys hanging off his scruffy jeans. He wore a black cowboy hat that covered his super short haircut, worn work boots and those mischief eyes. Seeing his boyish face hidden a little behind his ash brown beard made a flirty smile cross my lipsticked mouth. He had a charm about him, nice manners, let me order first and paid for my mocha. I could tell right away he was no push over and I was drawn to his confidence.

He asked if we could sit outside. I said yes and thought we were going to sit on the patio but instead he headed to his well-used work truck. He pulled down the somewhat rusted gate and we sat on the back for quite a while chatting. He was silly, telling me jokes he had made up. He asked me about myself but also managed to quickly tell me all of the instruments he played. We finished our coffees and I thought we might wrap up the evening but a short date was not in the cards for that night.

He asked if I wanted to hear him sing and play, because it just so happened that he had his guitar and harmonica with him. This was a dream come true for me. I loved hearing live music. The idea of being serenaded: stick a fork in me, I was done! He was a songwriter and all the songs were his originals. At that point in my life, I was quite impressed. We sat in the back of his pick-up, the sky moving in color from bright blue to lavender, orange, pink and finally black. He sang his funny or romantic songs while strumming and I ate it up, in disbelief. My ex hadn't been romantic the last few years of our marriage and I was desperate for some wooing. I felt surrounded in a warm blanket of romance and I had missed that feeling tremendously.

When he was done, I thought that would be the end of the date, which would have been fine with me, but no, he asked if I wanted to see a movie. There was a movie theater across the street so I figured we would go there. When I replied yes, I was seriously taken aback when he busted out with a movie screen and a projector! He set it all up in the parking lot in less than five minutes. I sat in the back of his truck in awe. I thought, where did this man come from and then, who cares as long as he's here with me. We ended up watching part of a black and white silent film where we both agreed the main star looked like Steven Colbert.

We got bored with the movie and he continued to sing more songs. I had to work at 8:45 the next morning and even though I didn't want to say goodnight, I knew I needed to. He walked me to my car and then asked if he could check it out because he had never been in a mini cooper before. I obliged because I was smitten with him by this point. We talked a bit more and then he gave me a hug goodbye. I really wasn't sure if I was going to hear from or see him again. I had thoroughly savored my time with him, but I wasn't sure if he had. At that point in the dating scene, I don't know why, but I would always, always doubt if the other person had a good time. The man spent hours with me, of course he had a good time! But, I had to obsess about it as I wrestled with sleep that night.

The next morning while I was at work, Phil did end up texting me a picture of the sunrise that I totally ate up. We made plans to meet a few days later at the boardwalk. It's not the place I would have chosen but when I first date someone I've been known to say yes to almost anything. We met in the parking lot, his guitar in tow, and walked around the bright lights, screams flying out of rides with the smell of churros in the air. He suggested eating on the wharf which is equally as touristy but luckily had better food.

We ate dinner at a fish house, then strolled on the pier, the wooden planks creaked under our feet. The smell of seaweed and sea lion songs in the background of our date. We sat on a bench so he could play a few songs under the stars, the waves crashing as backup singers. We then wandered to the beach where we dangled our legs out of a lifeguard station. It felt like hours, we talked and listened to one another. We spoke about our exes and I appreciated his compassion and open-mindedness. I honestly don't remember what else we said to one another, it was more the feeling and the way he looked into my eyes. He was there with a reassuring smile, listening to my sad tale, in the chilly, early September night. When we couldn't stand the cold any longer he walked me to my car and gave me another hug, still no kiss, and my mind wondered, does he like me just as a friend?

The following Sunday we spent the day driving up the coast, fog fading away to a sun filled sky. He showed me a tiny town where we tasted goat cheeses. On our way back we had a picnic on a cliff overlooking the Pacific Ocean. He pulled out a multi-colored Mexican blanket, we ate our sandwiches, chips and sparkling juices. When he brought out his guitar, a woman came by and asked if she could take our picture with her old fashioned black and white Polaroid camera. It looked like we were on a magic carpet ride, floating above the ocean, his cowboy hat and my sunglasses.

After baking in the sun for several hours we packed up and headed to my place. The song, "The Stand," by Joe Cocker came on as we headed south. He asked if I had ever heard this before. In those moments I noticed the 10 year age difference. Of course I knew this song and what it was about. But I didn't mind, it was good to have differences.

When we arrived at my place, I figured he would go but he asked if he could stay and watch a movie. He brought in his screen and projector and we started watching. It was quite a scene. We sat next to one another, a fluffy white dog behind us on the sofa, the other one, with short black and brown hair, slightly growling at him as one cat climbed over us back and forth. Then, as everyone started to settle into the movie, he put his right hand on my left cheek and he kissed me. I felt his rough facial hairs against my soft face, it was a new sensation. Then his hands moved to my neck and my breasts. His kisses were soft, then stronger and more forceful. I liked how his manual labored hands felt over my sundress and desired to feel them underneath it. I asked him to meet me in my room while I made sure the pets were taken care of.

When I entered my room he was standing naked against my double bed. Ok he wasn't totally naked he still had his cowboy hat on. At that point, I didn't have to wonder anymore if he liked me. There was clearly a part of his body that was very much excited about me.

He was a fun lover. We had sex on the kitchen table, oversized chair, in the garden, all over my bed, the floor and in many positions. He would say sweet things like how he liked how soft my hair was and then he would say nasty, sexy things, like how much he liked my big ass, while he spanked me. He was a very well-oiled sex machine and the stamina of his young age was priceless. He only spent the night once which was fine with me, I liked having the bed to myself.

One of the things I learned about myself and casual sex, that's what you get, casual sex. There was usually no snuggling after, no hand holding in public or introduction to each other's friends. I was so emotionally broken that I had no idea that I was completely incapable of intimacy.

The next week Phil invited me to go away with him for a weekend adventure but wouldn't tell me where. I was thrilled with the idea, my friends were shall I say, less than enthused. I kept getting calls and texts, "He's a stranger, where is he taking you," and "this could be dangerous, call us when you find out where you're going, when you get there and when will you be back." Their concern was quite sweet, it felt good to be looked after. But, I didn't let their worries make me nervous, I was in my fearless stage. Whenever I needed to push myself I just thought of all I went through with my ex and everything else was nothing to be scared of in comparison.

The day or middle of the night as it were, came and he picked me up at 4am. We took my mini because he only had his work truck. I know what you're thinking, but he paid for all the gas. I was reminded of his age when he wanted to leave at such an ungodly hour. He told me once we're all packed in the car that we were going to Lake Tahoe for a hot air balloon festival. The reason we had to leave so early was that they take off as the sun rises. I was thrilled, how fabulously fun! My ex would never have considered leaving early in the morning to see hundreds of brightly colored hot air balloons being released in the sky.

I became more awake instantly. That was good because he was exhausted. He had gotten no sleep and I with my five hours and new felt balloon launching excitement was ready and eager to drive. As we neared Sacramento, my eyes were not on the same page as my heart and we agreed to stop at a hotel. I paid for it for some reason, I know, I know, but he paid for everything else on the trip so I didn't feel like his sugar mama. We made our way up the eight floors, set our bags and jackets on the floor, stripped off our clothes and crawled in between the crisp white cotton sheets. The coolness of the sheets and softness of the bed was more than welcomed on my naked body. I was all ready to sleep, but he, a 28 year old man with a naked woman lying right next to him, was not. He wanted to have sex, of course he did and I loved every minute! I teased him about being too tired to drive, and he said this was different, he always had energy for sex. He had, unbeknownst to me brought along a full pack of Trojans and intended to make a large dent in the box. I liked how he would take charge and how much I excited him almost instantly.

We finally got to sleep as the sun came up and then continued to sleep until an hour before we had to leave. We had to have sex again, making our shower time extremely limited. But why take a long shower when you can have someone hot that wants you?

We checked out and ate at the hotel restaurant. We realized

we had missed the hot air balloons. We were both very go with the flow and although a bit disappointed, we came up with new ideas to entertain ourselves. We decided to continue north and look for natural hot springs. His spontaneous and relaxed nature was 180 degrees different from Jay, a cool breeze on a sweating face instead of a band aid stuck on a blistered toe.

We ended up going past Lake Tahoe and found a place where there were private rooms with natural hot mineral water. Another excuse to be naked around each other but this time with swirling warm water. Phil and I talked about all kinds of things, including coming up there next year for the festival. I don't think I had a noticeable physical reaction but I could tell my insides got all heated and I felt squirrely under my skin; he was talking about us in the future!

Why do we do that as humans, depend on future happiness instead of just being in the elation of a moment? It's like now isn't good enough. We have to know there is more to come. There really is only this moment and no guarantees about the next one. But I digress.

As he continued to talk casually about the next trip, my inner voice was having a field day. "Oh my god! He wants to come up here with me again and next year, what will we do in between, what other adventures will we go on? Is he seeing someone else? Will he only be seeing me by that point?" So on and so forth, it would not have mattered what he said I was convinced by that point that this relationship was definitely going somewhere. Once I finally quieted my inner voice I noticed he was gesturing to get out of the tub and to the wooden bench. The water was getting too hot for me and the bench seemed like a good place to cool off, but things just got hotter.

Not to be too graphic but I was on my period. It felt like he didn't even notice how messy things were. Blood dripped down my leg as he had me bent over the bench. I appreciated his nonchalant attitude, so different from what I was used to. Looking back it was pivotal in my own acceptance and joy in having sexual experiences while menstruating. Over time, I let go of all the taboo around it for myself and other women that I would be sexual with.

After getting cleaned up, Phil and I made our way towards home. He stopped the car on a whim and we found a walking path that took us to an open spot overlooking Lake Tahoe. The lake was humongous, brilliant blue almost the same color as the cloudless sky. The sun was starting to set and Phil ran back for his guitar and harmonica. He sang songs and we took pictures together for over an hour. It was quite romantic. My only problem, I wasn't in love with him. I imagined how awesome it would be if I was. I didn't dwell on it, and just delighted in being there with him, as we both were, until we drove home.

We went on a few more dates but it got bizarre, fast. On a phone call during my lunch break he confessed that he lived with someone. I never thought we were exclusive by any means but this was a little unsettling. He then went on to describe how he didn't pay any rent and was intimate with this woman who was significantly older. My guess was that she was in her early 60's, how do I know one might ask, well, because he asked if I wanted to meet her. He wondered if we could all do something sometime and I said, yes. At that point in my life I was at a place where I was open and saying yes to a lot of things.

So on a Wednesday night in October, I met them at "their" place before we went to the neighborhood pool hall. I had to enter a code to enter into an industrial complex. She was the manager of the storage facility so had an apartment on the property. I am saying this with as little judgement as possible, but I felt like I had walked into my grandmother's house.

I was immediately hit with a stale rose geranium scent and then my sight was accosted by lots and lots of doilies. If there was not a doily there was a fake flower or some sort of mish mashed floral print. There was too much furniture and a little dog, so ugly it was cute. When she came down the stairs, the first thing I noticed were her very long fake fingernails and red pants. To this day I think of her when I hear the song, "Mrs. Robinson," by Simon and Garfunkel. But she was no Ann Bancroft. I know how this sounds but she was very sweet and incredibly nervous. I just couldn't believe I was having sex with the same man that she was. I mean, he was at least 30 years younger than her. Then I thought about her, "If you can get it, you go girl!" It was such a weird situation. She offered me a coke and I said, "No thank you, I'm fine." We were all on our best awkward behaviors.

Getting to know her that night, I learned that she had been terribly abused by her ex-husband and Phil had been a shiny star in her life. I know he had helped me too. What the two of us had in common was this divorcee angel of sex.

After our "date", he walked me to my car and the next day

asked what I thought of her. I said that she was nice but that I was dating him, not them. He never said anything but I think he was hoping for a threesome relationship.

After that conversation he cancelled plans. I was having an art show, the first time my art was displayed with First Fridays in a store downtown, a huge deal for me. I didn't expect him to come but he didn't even call or text me that day or that weekend. After that I didn't want to waste my time. He asked me to go out on a Tuesday night and I said I wasn't interested in being a mid-week booty call. I was fine hanging out anytime but one of the days needed to be a Friday or Saturday night and a date. He said ok and I didn't hear from him for over a week.

The last straw was when he left me a message on a Friday to see if I could hang out on that next Monday. I waited until Monday and sent him a text message. I know, terrible manners, but I had already told him my feelings. He hadn't listened so my "so long Charlie" text stated that I had cherished my time with him and now it was done. His response was a little surprised and that there was more fun to be had but ok.

It was fun while it lasted and I liked the little bit of romance but I had decided I was nobody's back up, or Tuesday afterthought. This dating experience helped me to my realization, I wanted all or nothing at that point, or so I thought. My many affairs after proved otherwise.

To put a funny ending to this tartly tale, a few months later, I was hiking with some friends in the redwoods. As we turned a corner I heard a guitar and saw a black cowboy hat. I could not see his face, but I knew it was Phil. I recognized the boots and the giant key ring as I quickly walked by. He was there with some young thing, I saw the gaze that must have been on my face months prior. I let out a chuckle. I realized that being the sweet guitar playing songwriter was his shtick. Too funny!

Adonis

Have you ever had sex with someone that you never in your wildest dreams thought you would? Someone with such a fantastic body, soft hair, full lips, eyes that you tumble into, just everything that you have fantasied about? That was Adonis to me. Not only did I meet him on the fetish website, so he was kinky, but he also worked with differently-abled teens and had eyes the color of where the sky meets the ocean at dusk. He had just enough stubble, that 5 o'clock shadow to be mysterious and sexy. His voice was even dreamy. Oh and he was maybe 27 years old.

On election night 2012 it was not what I was doing, but whom. I was scrolling through the bios of over 100 locals when a Greek god specimen came across my screen. All of his pictures were scenes he created. He had poses and titled them like, "the nerd," or "the lover." His creativity was not only funny but enticing. I sent him a message after looking at the pictures and reading his bio. I was thrilled that he didn't have pictures of his penis, only of his created scenes.

About two minutes later I heard a bing, he had written me back! We agreed to meet at a local coffee shop. When I walked in, I knew it was him the moment our eyes met. He was kind of shy and nervous which I found endearing. He was definitely younger than me, very fit and there was not just mischievousness but kindness behind his eyes. He paid for my coffee and we made small talk for a bit. We then ended up walking around for hours and he told me about his brothers, his cats, his job. We both talked a lot and it was easy. I completely forgot that the presidential election was taking place. When we finally got back to my car I offered him a ride to his car and when he sat down he said sure but was also wondering if we'd like to continue the date. Well hello, are you kidding me?!? The answer was most definitely YES. I drove him to his car and he asked for my number in case we got separated.

Adonis followed me to my studio and once we got in the door he started taking his clothes off. Man, did that guy have a killer body! WOW! I have to admit I was a little intimidated by how smooth and muscular he was but I didn't need to be. He was enthusiastic about my body and we appreciated one another all over my bed.

Being new at the sex with strangers I didn't really know what to do afterwards. I offered him to stay but earned that wasn't the thing to do with online casual hookups. So, I walked him out to his car and said we should do it again. We didn't contact each other; but I guess we had a November thing because he came over in November 2013, even though there was no election that night, it was even better than the previous November! I happened to see him at the bar he used to work at when I was there with some friends to listen to a band. He was still gorgeous and smiled at me with those dreamy hazel eyes. I decided to send him a text to invite him over for some more adult fun. It was late by then so I went to sleep. I woke up the next morning with a text from him that he would like to see me again.

He came over to my house the following Tuesday night. It was around the holidays so I met him at the door in my naughty Ms. Claus outfit. I put on my black lace thong underwear, fishnet stockings, and black corset and then slipped the red velvety Santa short suit over me. The final touch were the fuck-me high heeled black leather boots. When he arrived he was pleasantly surprised by my outfit. We discussed his latest adventure of being a submissive (sub) and his realization that he was more of a dominant (dom). In my little baby toe dip into the BDSM world I realized I was most definitely a sub. His realization worked out perfectly for us. I did remember from our previous encounter that he had a fantasy of being totally naked while the woman was fully clothed so I pulled him into my bedroom. I took off all of his clothes and had my way with him. His body had only gotten more firm, his hair softer in between my fingers and his tongue more talented in my mouth. He was a generous lover. We both felt fantastic after our hours together and I reveled in our conversation after as he held me against his Greek god of a body.

Years later I saw him again for a couple of months. I believe we would have had many more encounters but my lack of self-confidence, while first dating, prohibited it. I felt like he was "out of my league," which was not true. He ended up texting me to start things up again. I was very pleasantly surprised and on our third attempt at a friends with kinky benefits, we delved into many areas sexually that I had barely even heard of, let alone tried. I felt safe with him. I knew it wouldn't last, he was so much younger and when I was really ready for a relationship, I knew it would be with a butch woman. After our amazing adventures, we mutually agreed to be friends without the kinky benefits. I hoped he found someone as sweet and sexy as he was.

The Captain

So, I did it again; a crush on someone that I met on a dating site. I had told myself that I was done dating for a while, that I just wanted to concentrate on myself and I did, but then he appeared. His name was Dave and we had a very flirty texting exchange for an evening. He sent me a fun text the following morning and then disappeared. When he texted me a month later I was irritated and didn't text him back for a week. I was like, what is up with this dude?

He finally asked me out for a casual dinner on a Friday night. I wasn't sure if I should go as he had been so flaky the month prior. I decided to go for it, we had a lot in common and he was silly and smart, a bonus. He picked me up and we went out to sushi. He dared me to put this huge end piece of a roll in my mouth and I almost got it all, but not quite. We dared each other back and forth.

After dinner, we drove to the beach for a little while and then went back to my place. He gave me a full body massage that was so gentle and sincere. He then proceeded to fling me around my bed, all masculine and rough. Yes, we did have sex a few times that night and it was fantastic. After, we ate vanilla ice cream with olla berry sauce. He then put his head in my lap and ended up falling asleep. I could just see the side of his face, the dark brown stubble on his strong jaw line, the shape of his closed eyes, and felt the warmth exude from his body. The hair of his beard was not prickly but smooth, I can't really describe why I liked it so much, but I did. I breathed in his after-sex scent, heard his heartbeat, and tasted him on my lips. His arm underneath mine, trusting me. I embraced who his was in those moments.

He ended up waking up around 2am and had to go home for his dog, daffodil. He texted me when he got home that he didn't die, that it was nice to meet me (with a smiley face) and hoped I had a good night. I didn't respond until the next morning where I thanked him for letting me know he got home safe.

A few weeks later at his request I arrived at the Captain's house. I called him the Captain because he had been in the Navy. Earlier he had sent me a text that he wanted to hone his massage skills and he was also in need of a shower due to his biweekly Thursday night haircut. I was a willing participant for the shower and the massage. I was planning on going to the gym and didn't want to give that up so I showed up to his house in my gym clothes with my neck and back sweaty. What did I care, we were taking a shower first, right?

The Captain gave me a hug and a kiss after his adorable dog said hello with lots of kisses. I was given the honor of her presenting me with her toy elephant. I wanted to date him for his dog, but decided to keep that one to myself since that was my first time there. He showed me around, offered me a drink as we looked outside at the semi-dark back yard.

I suddenly was very aware that I was in my gym clothes on our second date. I made apologies for being all sweaty. He was totally relaxed about it. The Captain then led the way to his bathroom, I was pleasantly surprised at how clean it was. He had a vanilla smelling candle burning and I couldn't help myself and looked around for any signs of a woman living there. It really was a bachelor pad but I was impressed with his skin and hair products. I looked on the bathroom counter and noticed the piece de resistance. "Do you really have a gigantic bottle of lavender bubble bath for yourself?" He replied, "Yes I do, I like to take care of myself." The Captain became so much more attractive to me at that point.

First his shirt came off, then my sweater, bra and jeans. I struggled to take off his belt which was an American flag (I overlooked it in my urgency) and he helped, "Pull on the stars, they release the buckle." "Pull on the stars," he was cracking me up. Now most of our clothes were on the floor and we stood there staring at each other in our underwear. I appreciated that the Captain didn't wear tightie whities. I never saw the draw in that. I admit I was a little afraid after the flag belt buckle but luckily he had on blue boxers.

I noticed the rubber duck out of the corner of my eye and I grinned thinking of the silly picture he had sent me. He had been in glasses, in the morning, his hair sticking up and mouth wide open holding the rubber ducky with horns. The shower water was gratifyingly steamy, the way I liked it. I let the Captain get all the way under it first, the droplets caught on his hazelnut chest hair and it felt even hotter in there. He grabbed the body gel and rubbed the liquid in between his chunky strong hands. I didn't know what exactly we were doing and then he turned me around to lather my back. He soaped my entire body, lavender bubbles cascaded down while he gave me a back massage. I was in awe, just trying to take it all in, present in the sudsy delight.

After we both rinsed off, I thought we were done, but oh no, he then wet my hair and ran his manly hands through my blond waves. He massaged my scalp with shampoo and then conditioner, I melted. I tried to remember the last time I had bathed with someone else and not only bathed but had someone wash, shampoo and condition my hair. Oh goodness, I was in trouble.

After that we didn't see each another in almost two months. I figured he wasn't interested anymore. We still communicated 3-5 times a week but no physical contact. I decide to be brave and asked him if he was still interested in seeing me. I expressed there would be no hard feelings, I just desired open communication. He immediately got back to me and said he most definitely did want to keep seeing me but that the holidays were busy and difficult.

He said he wanted to be there emotionally and physically so I could have the whole package. I was so tempted to capitalize on "the package" part of the sentence but since he was sounding very genuine I didn't want to sound like a perv. He also said that I was sweet, warm and that he felt great around me. I was happy with that answer and replied that I wanted to continue seeing him as well.

Two nights later I received a text that he was watching the movie, "The Way," and he had all kinds of questions about the Camino. I was out with a friend and didn't get it until an hour later. I texted him back and didn't expect a reply but he ended up speaking very open and intimately with me. That night he had tried to go to his company winter party, drove there but couldn't go in alone. I told him I was available if he wanted to talk about it and he did.

We both expressed how hard it was to be divorced. You wish the dream, the illusion, still existed. He expressed he didn't want her back. He wished it had never fallen apart in the first place. I understood that all too well. The difference, I didn't wish for it to be any different. What good does that do? To have regrets, to wish for something that didn't happen. It is wasted energy and told him I liked to focus on the present as you can't change the past.

I continued to see the Captain off and on for a few years, we became more friends than anything. We would text each other about the women we were seeing and occasionally have a platonic burger together. We both were travelers and loved to hear about one another's journeys. He has a baby now and is so content being a devoted dad. I'm truly happy for him. He deserves the bliss he has created in his life.

SF Aaron

I thought I would try online dating again, for like the hundredth time, you know if third time isn't the charm than 100 has to be right? So I found out about a new dating site that was like a game. There were pictures of men or women or both if you preferred. You swipe your finger to the right if you like them or left if you don't. It's shallow and based of their picture with a little paragraph of what they like, if they wrote something.

At first you might think it is horrible but honestly in online dating everyone's main focus is how the other person looks. If people deny it they're lying and I'd rather people be up front. I decided to sign up for it and see what would happened. I went back and forth on looking at just men, then just women, then both, then back to just men. Over ninety percent of the women on there were too feminine or hadn't liked me back. When they did 'like' me they didn't start conversations and most of the time when I did they didn't write back or weren't engaging, to say the least!

Men were much more forward and I appreciated that. I talked to this guy one night but then he 'unliked' me, I guess that's what you would call it. In the morning he had disappeared. However, I woke up to a message from a man in San Francisco who said he wanted to be my oral sex slave. Let me tell you this is not something I had ever been offered. I was a little shocked only because I wasn't on the fetish website. On this guy's profile he talked about watching foreign films, eating out and taking a drive in his Porsche. He sounded a little bit like a douchebag but he called me "Goddess," and again this is not a popular thing I had been called.

My response to him was if he was going to be my sex slave before or after the movie and the Porsche drive? He responded right back with, "Both." He also said he'd like to take me shopping for sex toys, shoes, outfits and especially he wanted me to make him buy a collar and leash for him.

I had so much fun looking online for stuff, the most interesting part was as I was looking at black and blue, and then he messaged me that he'd like pink and sparkly! I am usually very open about gender, I couldn't believe how stereotypic

I was with the colors. I was even more disgusted with my-self because at first I didn't like that he wanted pink! Ahhh! I thought about it and all of it was new, exciting and sexy to me. We messaged back and forth pictures (I don't send naked pictures and luckily neither did he.) He did send a picture without his shirt and with pink bunny ears and a pink collar. I wasn't quite expecting it but rolled with it. We then agreed to meet the next Thursday night.

I still can't believe I drove to San Francisco on a Thursday night for a booty call, a kinky oral sex slave booty calls; oh yeah, that was why. I meet him at a local bar in the Sunset district which was very close to the ocean. He bought me a drink and we made small talk. He was cute and there was some chemistry there. We finished our drinks and then I drove us to his place because it was so close he had walked. He owned a cute house and several nice cars, I assumed because they were all covered. He even had a backyard which was hard to come by in San Francisco. Honestly, none of that actually mattered to me. I didn't care how much money he or anyone I dated had, as long as they were kind, fun, sexy and adored me.

We chatted for a few minutes, he offered me juice or water and then asked if I was interested in messing around. I figured that's why I was there. He asked if I liked kissing and I answered honestly, very much so. Being naked and having sex with someone I had just met was still awkward to me. I was used to being in a relationship, and knowing my partners likes and dislikes. Aaron started kissing me and he was a good enough kisser.

We started undressing and then he asked to wear my stockings and booty shorts. It was something that no man had ever done with me and I thought I liked it. The best part was that he was an awesome oral sex slave. I realized that however intriguing being a dominatrix might be to me, I do not like being mean. I am nice in bed. I'm not boring by any means but I don't like being forceful or telling people what to do. I am a bottom, sub, however you want to describe. I am not the dominant lover. So, the sex was good and I valued it all except for the part after we said good bye. I surprised myself driving home because I started sobbing. I couldn't hide from myself that I had feelings for someone else.

14

Back to The Camino

I sat on a hotel bed in Leon, Spain. I was actually in a converted attic and hotter than if I was staying in the devil's deluxe suite in Hades, if one believed in such a place. Miserable did not begin to describe my mood. I had gotten lost and was wandering around in the dark, unfamiliar, small town for at least an hour when I finally found the tiny hotel. Sweaty from fear, I just wanted to get in my room. Once there I had hoped it would have cooled down, it was midnight. Nope. I hadn't found a *launderia* so after taking a quick blessedly cool shower, I hand washed my black toe socks, travel panties and bras in the sink, with my thin sheets of laundry soap from REI.

I was exhausted. I turned out all the lights, except the bathroom. I had developed a dread of the dark since leaving my marriage. It was a feeling of claustrophobia. I had occasionally been waking up in panic attacks so I would leave on a light. If I was in the dark I felt like I couldn't breathe. I believe all the years of feeling confined in my marriage manifested into the panic attacks. I didn't have them in the day but would wake up in one. It hadn't happened since the first night on the Camino where I was locked in, but I wanted to prevent one, if I could.

I succumbed to the day and laid down on the warm sheets, the semi-darkness and the knowing that I would be on a train in the morning. I was headed to the last stop on the Camino De Santiago where one is able to get the appropriate stamps in order to get *the compostela* (certificate of completion for walking The Way of St. James.) I was unable to sleep. I just kept thinking about how I didn't want to take a train to Sarria. I was done walking, but how could I be? Beads of shame rolled down my face disguised as sweat mixed with tears. The Camino was around 500 miles/780 kilometers and I had barely walked 100 miles.

I had taken a modern art, titanium swirl filled side trip to Bilbao. I had wanted to see Frank Gehry's masterpiece ever since I had heard of its creation a decade prior. From there, I hopped back on a train to Burgos to see the second largest cathedral in Spain. I was not a religious person but I felt drawn to see it as part of my quest.

I was drawn to Leon because they were known for their cathedral as well. I felt I was already "cheating" the Camino by taking a train in between these towns and then horror of horrors, only going to walk the last 100 kilometers from to Sarria to Santiago. I laid there feeling like a fraud, like a charlatan. I felt like I was the worst person on earth, a liar to my friends and that I lacked integrity. I always kept my promises and did what I said I would do. Ever since I found out about my wife's infidelity, integrity was more important to me than anything else. And now I was just as guilty, wasn't I? If I didn't at least walk the last part of the Camino how could I show my face to anyone that I knew?

Most importantly, how could I tell Hannah and Matt after all those hours of training, the days in REI, and the miles on the treadmill at the gym? I was a failure, I would be a failure if I did what my soul truly yearned for. I couldn't even compose the thought. I continued to lay there for hours picturing all the little beds and random people I would have had to share a room with, their odd noises and smells. I didn't want to do that. I didn't think one should have to put up with another's snoring if they weren't your lover; especially after walking ten to fifteen miles, carrying everything on your back. I realized what a spoiled American I was. Running out of things to chastise myself for, naked in self-loathing and damp sheets. I looked at the digital clock hoping for some solace. The florescent green digits that displayed 3:30 were not that. The clock had no answer. It was only getting nearer when I had to wake up from no sleep to get on a train to go somewhere I didn't want to go.

In a moment of pure desperation I finally broke down and asked myself what I had wanted to ask for days but was too full of fear to do. "If you could do anything, go anywhere, what would you do?" My answer was immediate, "Stop walking, go to Santiago and wander throughout Spain for the remaining 3 and ½ weeks." In that second I knew that I was in charge of my own life and could do whatever I wanted! I had, of course, always known that but my ego was finally broken down enough to let my higher self be heard. I had to let go of all of the self-conflicted hate and shame. I had to have the courage to tell people my truth and that truth was that my Camino, my path was not just the one of St. James.

I made up my mind. I would follow my heart and change my train ticket to go directly to Santiago. As soon as I let go of the judgements, I was asleep. The next thing I remember, the sun shone on my smile as I turned off my alarm. I was conscious of how much I had been tormenting myself to keep on the walk. I was living a life that I thought I had wanted but it turned out I changed my mind. That is one of life's blessings that I have experienced; we get to change whenever we want! Instead of continuing with the feelings of the last few days, getting lost, edgy and just not feeling right in my own skin, as soon as I followed my heart, everything was easy. I found everything tasted better, people were friendlier and I located where I was going without effort.

When I called the place I was drawn to stay in Santiago they had a room and because it was the same day there was a special where I got breakfast included in the price! As I boarded the train to Santiago I knew it was not an ending of The Camino but the beginning of my new adventure.

Santiago

After months spent in preparation, climbing up the Pyrenees in the rain and down in the hail, swollen ankles, full bladder with no cover in sight and pride in the knowing I carried everything I needed to survive on my back, I had made it to Santiago. Years in the making, I had reached my destination. I stood there, salty water sneaking out from underneath my black sunglasses. The sun heating my blushed face, tired calf muscles and mud splattered boots.

It was supposed to be my final destination but would be the heart instead. Saturday, May 3, 2014, was the day I attended the pilgrims mass in Santiago, Spain. The day was weeks sooner than I had planned. My original goal was to walk all 500 miles in my dependable dark blue and lavender hiking boots, the cool spring wind blowing through my short dyed blond hair, sweat seeping from my armpits against my trusty pack straps, as I explored Northern Spain on foot. I was supposed to experience the Camino that way. I had traveled many miles on foot, close to 100, squished into taxis, witnessed the countryside whiz by on a train or as I listened to American pop music on a bus. How could I have known that a new adventure would call to me five nights prior in the Leon hotel? That night I heard my soul's song. It had to scream at me because I was so stubborn but finally at 3am I let it sink in. The Camino de Santiago was only the beginning of The Camino de Labris.

I had dreamt of how this day would unfold since watching a matinee showing of "The Way," on an October day in 2011. I had saved money from working at the dental office, purchased items like a travel wallet, sun-screen treated shirts, a foot care module and pants that converted to shorts. I had hiked tree covered hills that I thought I'd need my asthma inhaler for, and spent countless muggy hours at the gym for the last year to make this pilgrimage. I was finally going to be in the presence of Saint James' Cathedral in Santiago, Spain. To say it was a dream come true wasn't big enough. I had survived my separation, my mediation meetings and divorce. Being in that town on that day was a glorious triumph, like winning an Olympic medal, Purple Heart and college degree all wrapped up in one personal accomplishment.

Being able to attend the Pilgrim's mass was an honor I on the one hand didn't know if I deserved and on the other knew that I was a pilgrim, not of Saint James' Way, but my way. After about 15 minutes walking, there it was, the giant cathedral reaching up to the sky in honor of one of Jesus' apostles. I felt like harps should be playing and a spot light from heaven (if you believe in such a place) should be shining down on it.

I had come all that way and was going to the mass. I was going in the cathedral to experience what I had imagined for years. I felt privileged to be there and to find a seat in the second to last row. Looking around I saw many *Peregrinos* and also families of the people who lived in the small town. I had only been on my own without my friends for 3 days, but as the mass began and the part where you shake hands or hug your neighbor happened, I welled up with emotion.

The idea of being kind to people you don't know became vital. I really had no idea how much a smile from a stranger could mean to me until just then. I didn't know anyone in that town but the people who didn't even speak my language were such a comfort; their warmth dancing out of their smiles. I belonged. It didn't matter that I did not understand the mass. When the giant urn with incense was pushed by six priests swung above my head, I was a deserving pilgrim. I had seen the urn ritual in the movie and had been in anticipation of it since. Looking up at its brass handles as it swung over me can only be described as a full body and soul blessing.

Fairly filled with courage after the mass I decided to attempt to get at least a stamp from the cathedral for my pilgrim's passport. In the pilgrims passport you get stamps from all the towns you visit. You can get them from where you stay, eat, churches, stores, etc. I was advised to go to the pilgrim's office.

I noticed it right away as a line of people were snaked around the stone building. I approached it with uncertainty, but got in line. I still felt a little like I didn't deserve to be there. I was told by my friend Matt that the Camino officials were very strict on how you earn your compostella. The compostella is the documentation that you completed the pilgrimage. To get the compostella you need to have at least 2 stamps from each of the towns from at least the last 100 kilometers of the pilgrimage. I had walked more than that amount, but at the beginning, including over the Pyrenees Mountains but I didn't have a single stamp from the last 100 kilometers.

I noticed a woman with the pilgrim's office checking everyone's pilgrim's passports. My heart beat so loudly that I thought the Italian bicyclists in their speedos must have surely heard it. When it was my turn, I walked up to her with my big California smile and she politely smiled back speaking to me in English. She asked where I was from as she thumbed through my passport, then stopped and looked at me, left eyebrow raised. I knew what she was going to say and so before she spoke I blurted out, "I'm hoping to just get a stamp." Her reply was not unkind, "They might give you a stamp, might."

And she handed me back my passport while I waited behind the glee filled bicyclists, no doubt that their compostellas were eminent.

I witnessed one by one, pilgrims come out of the office proudly waiving their proof. I was envious and a little disappointed in myself. But, then I remembered I had chosen to walk my way. My pilgrimage was not only of St. James and would continue the following day on a train to Madrid.

My nerves started to do a jig on my psyche, what would the clerk say, would they kick me out? Would people point, stare, scowl or worse, laugh? Numerous embarrassing scenarios played out in my head as I waited for my turn. A few minutes later, I was waived to the second man behind the counter. My eyes were drawn to his tiny welcoming smile. I smiled back anxiously as he asked for my pilgrim's passport. While he peered at it I admitted, "I didn't finish." He looked up at me and in Spanish said, "Finnistere?" I replied "no," (Finnistere was also called the "End of the World," on the west coast of Spain, a lot of pilgrims go there or to Muxia after the Camino.) I then tried to explain that I did not complete the walk and that I only wanted a stamp from the cathedral for my passport. With his Spanish accent he said, "It's ok," handed me a clip board and asked for my regular passport. I did not understand what was happening. Why would he need my passport and these statistics? I read and answered every line in a state of confusion. The form wanted my name, age, sex, country of origin, the reason I walked the Camino. I gave him the completed information and he handed me back my regular passport. He then showed me the stamp from the cathedral as he handed my pilgrims passport back to me. I sighed a sigh of relief, satisfied to receive the green statue stamp. Then, time slowed down as he stood up and his right hand presented another document. He handed me my compostella. It was written all in Latin. Black type covered the cream colored parchment with a vibrant portrait of Saint James on the upper right hand side. As I scrolled down the page in utter disbelief and amazement, at the bottom he had handwritten my name, Labris Marie Willendorf with the date, May 3, 2014 and his signature. I couldn't move. I was in the middle of a miracle.

15

The Camino De Labris

In wonder and awe for the rest of the day, I wandered around Santiago. Everything was brighter and I felt I could achieve anything I set my soul on. My self-confidence grew in leaps and bounds.

I had another path that led not just to Santiago but to Madrid, Valencia, Mallorca and Barcelona. From Santiago all I knew was that I needed to be by the sea. I was homesick, yet not wanting to leave Spain, so water was my home, my comfort. I looked on a map of *Espana* and saw Valencia. Momentarily, I pondered going to Portugal but when I listened to my gut I knew my trip was about experiencing Spain. I decided on Valencia but I had to transfer trains in Madrid so I thought I'd stay there for three nights. Sleeping somewhere different every night was harder on my emotional and physical health then I thought it would be. On The Camino the most I had stayed was two nights somewhere so three nights in Madrid was the least I wanted to do. The sea was calling and I knew I needed to stay in Valencia longer. I booked an Airbnb apartment for eight days. In Madrid, I had chosen a hotel that was pretty close to the train station. I really had no idea where I was going or what I was going to do there. I had planned to be on the Camino for six weeks and found myself with three and a half weeks to wander. I was so excited and also a little terrified. I had never been on a trip in a foreign country not knowing a soul.

I reached my hotel in Madrid in the evening and the only place open that wasn't fast food and within walking distance was a little bar/restaurant where I ordered a steak, French fries and wine, not very Spanish but tasty. I went back to my room and tried to plan out my following day by looking at Things to Do in Madrid on Google. Having a Smartphone was like having my own private tour guide. I fell asleep to ideas of Flamenco, tapas and Picasso.

The next morning I woke up and it was the first morning since arriving in Europe that I didn't know where my hiking shoes would take me. I was fine. Then I wasn't. Panic snuck up on me like a fever. A flood of knowledge that I knew no one and nothing in this place spread though my entire body. I lay in my queen bed for I don't know how long. I kept looking at my phone like it would tell me the answers to all my questions and squelch my fear but goddamnit, that vertical line on the google search bar just kept blinking at me, like I was supposed to know what to search for!

My mind had a field day, "What are you doing here in this country, here in Spain, alone, not knowing where anything is? Your Spanish isn't even that good, *aye dios mio! Muy loca chica!*" I just laid there in the white sheets thinking maybe I'd just stay in bed all day, no one would know the difference. I didn't know what I was going to do. I didn't know, except that I would know if I stayed in bed all day, in this dark room, telling myself mean things.

Finally, I quieted the chattering in my mind and in the blackout curtained room asked myself, "Can I do this?" The answer: "Get up and take a shower." I thought, yes, I like taking showers. Showers are something I know how to do. I then remembered my friend Stella told me about the Reina Sofia Museum. She told me Picasso's, "Guernica" was there and that I had to see it while I was in Madrid. I put my achy feet on the beige carpet and headed toward the bright bathroom. I told myself, just take the shower, put the shampoo in your right hand then put it in your hair, rinse under the lovely warm water, now condition, rinse and wash your body, you can do this.

After showering, I got ready. I realized I only had hiking clothes. I desperately wanted a pair of jeans, some hair gel, pink lipstick and mascara. I felt quite proud of myself, I had walked somewhere between 80-100 miles, carrying everything on my back without any hair product or makeup. Full disclosure, I did have a red tinted Chap Stick that I wore on my 39th birthday but that was as feminine as it got.

I felt like now was the time for some girliness. I picked up my phone again and this time I did know what to search for: a MAC store. I didn't find one but there was a Sephora, not too far away. I could get everything in one place because there was an H&M near there too for clothes; victory was mine. The shower had done wonders and I felt prepared for lots of directions when I reached the concierge but when I asked how to get to the metro he pointed across the street. I had no idea that

I had picked such a convenient place to stay. In that moment I knew the next 3 and ½ weeks were going to be incredible.

Madrid was an awesome city known for many things, including, Flamenco. I thoroughly enjoyed wandering the streets looking at shops, open markets and eating tapas! After finding femme clothes, etc. I took Stella's advice and was mesmerized by Picasso's, "Guernica." It is something one needs to witness in person. Art as genius and madness. I was then inspired to by myself a ticket to a Flamenco show. I couldn't be in Madrid and not see a show. That same day my cousin on my mother's side, messaged me that our great grandmother was born there. I had no idea!

Celebrating my connection to this beautiful Spanish city, I got dressed in my only black dress and headed to the small theater. Inside the theater there were small tables where you picked your own seat. I sat in the second row. I am so grateful that I did. Flamenco was powerful. I had no idea of its depth. The music, voices and movements reached in and grabbed me. The struggles, traditions and splendor of the Andalusian Roma (Gypsies) captivated me for the hours I was there. The music still gets to me on the rare occasion I hear that Spanish guitar.

After my three days of exploring and reconnecting to my ancestry, I knew I was ready for my next city. Valencia was all about seeing the Mediterranean and living in a place for more than three nights. I had walked so many miles across Northern Spain and had been away from my giant blue Pacific Goddess for more than three weeks. I loved the comforts of home in California but the thrill of adventure and not knowing the abundance the next day had to offer was what propelled me.

Traveling and exploring, delving my fingers into the cool damp earth, seeing gigantic pillars of fruit on a basilica, attempting to converse with native speakers in my broken tongue or discovering the scent of century old bakeries, was what my soul yearned for. I felt I could get inside myself more, figure out who I was with each place I explored. If I stayed somewhere at least one week I could get to know it, feel it in my marrow.

So, I collected everything from my hotel in Madrid, flung my pack on and headed to the train station I arrived in. I left in plenty of time, so I wouldn't have any stress.

Once I arrived in the station, I kept looking for my train number. I thought maybe it wasn't shown as I was early. Time kept passing and trains after were lighting up on the board. I couldn't understand what was going on. I kept looking at my ticket, it was the correct day and time and... not the correct station! I had completely forgot that one of the reasons I had decided to go to Madrid was that I had to switch stations to go to Valencia.Oops! I tried to rush to the right station but there was not enough time. Luckily, there were several trains to Valencia so I would only be a couple hours later. My host in Valencia was laid back and asked me to text her when I was in town. Ah the wonders of being an inexperienced traveler.

Leaving it on a Valencian Beach

I arrived outside the apartment building I would be sharing and I met Malinka, the 30 year old, married, blond Ukrainian woman around 3pm. When she saw my 30+lb backpack, she offered to help me up the stairs. She said there was no elevator and in this moment I realized I was not done hiking. Even though I had left the Camino, my adventure was continuing now I was on a different path, right in front of me, nine stories high.

My fifth day in Valencia I decided to go to the beach alone, Malinka was a great hostess and we wandered together a lot of the time. She had gotten me to try blood sausage, taught me how to use public transportation and become more comfortable with partial nudity because she walked around mostly naked to and from the bathroom we shared. She also loved to go topless around the house. I didn't mind at all. She wasn't my type but I'm not going to say no to seeing boobs. But, on this day I felt I needed my own time.

I walked the five minutes to the cream, sandy beach with translucent turquoise water and sat down with my straw mat, water bottle and music. I put on the audio version of an Eckhart Tolle book and began to inhale the mist, coconut sunscreen and bizarre body odor of passersby. I was alive there. I observed the women in all of their voluptuous or slender bodies, some in one piece suits, others in bikinis or topless. They all appeared at peace in their skin whether it be marshmallow or mocha. There was a feeling not only of acceptance but of celebration of their bodies. As I surveyed the women, I acknowledged my entire adulthood, I had done an excellent job of keeping the chubby, sad little child hidden and silent inside. I was learning about living in the Now. With closed eyes, I welcomed my inner child out. I took her hand with a soft, confident grip and we held one another in the Spanish sunlight. I expressed how beautiful she was and always had been. I looked into the confused milk chocolate eyes and was not only 39 and 7 but also 29, 16, and 11.

I relived the middle school bullying, being picked last for any sports team. The doctor's office scale came next, and then a department store where sizes stopped at "8". I felt the societal pressure and self-shame layer upon layer of fat and years. The coats of disgrace had not merely lacquered and stained my body but the thickness had spread into my mind and worse, slowly penetrated my spirit. The memories came of being told I was fat by other children, or sensing the thought by the not-so-subtle arched eyebrows followed by the disappointment in the only clothes offered in my size.

Breathing all of my pieces, I sat there, feet grounded in the warm sand and took it all. I filled myself with all those years, all those emotions until I was a tornado of past pain engulfed to my core. And then it was done. I exhaled, surrendered all of it over to the Spanish sky. The Mediterranean waters cleansed all the places that had been covered in that slime of shame. Pale skin now glistening, how much lighter we all were. Beholding all of me, I stood up, held hands and not only forgave my own cruelty, but was filled for the first time with self-acceptance and adoration of my soft stomach rolls and thick thighs. Glowing, I released my younger selves. I watched as they giggled, and skipped back to the past, leaving the 39 year old on her mat to revel in my size 14 paisley blue bikini. Agony and humiliation not inside anymore, I had expelled them. I blew the girls and women each a kiss and turned back to begin rejoicing in every inch I occupied in the world.

The Magic of Mallorca

After nine fantastic days in Valencia, I had decided to splurge for a nice hotel room on the island of Mallorca for four days. When I walked into my room, the hundreds of dollars spent were easily accounted for. I was surrounded by crisp, white linens, energetic deep turquoise walls with bursts of tangerine. Everything was clean, bright and contemporary, my favorite design style. My bed could have fit four of me. I sprawled out across it and could see the sun shining on the Mediterranean Sea through my glass balcony door. I could gaze out at the seawater while sipping a glass of Mistella, a sweet Spanish white wine. I felt like I should be on Lifestyles of the Rich and Famous, well if it were the '90's, I suppose! Part of me just wanted to stay there the entire long weekend and soak it all in, but the island was serenading me to come out and play.

I made arrangements to go hot air ballooning and cave exploring. On the surface those sound adventurous and exciting things to do by oneself and they absolutely were, but it was more about the feeling underneath. In my marriage we always asked each other if we could do things. It started out as sweet but then got twisted and turned into another controlling tool she kept in her hip belt for me. There was always the excuse of never enough money for things. I had asked her about hot air ballooning for years but that was much too frivolous for our finances. It was also in the way she said things or implied them. It was like I didn't want a house and nice things, if I also wanted to go out of town for a weekend. I didn't understand why we couldn't have it all. She had convinced me after the first couple of years of being together to get a joint bank account. This sounds logical and lots of couples do that, but before meeting her I was fiercely independent and the idea of sharing my money was the last thing I would have done.

Once she had been irritated about my purchase of stationary, why couldn't I write letters on regular paper? My first instinct was regret that I had bought the stationary but then the feisty part of me retorted, "And how much do you spend on cigarettes every week?" She just looked at me, smiled sheepishly, yea I won that one. But I didn't like being that way, the tit for tat, making her feel bad because I felt bad. That was all nonsense. As the time went by I had begun caving in to little things, like saying ok to the same account or not eating certain foods because she didn't like them. I didn't travel because she was afraid of flying. I'm not saying it was all bad but that pressure was a mountain, it didn't matter that it was once covered in vibrant wild flowers and brilliant green grass, it was a mountain, and now it had vanished from my back.

The notion that I didn't have to ask anyone's permission to spend my money any longer meant I was my own person again. Did I spend it frivolously sometimes? You bet your ass I did and enjoyed every second! When I was up in that yellow and red giant balloon with ten strangers, the Spanish wind in my hair, the independence of it was priceless. Watching the sun come up over the Mediterranean, a new day beginning, I felt the dawning of my freshly reclaimed heart as well.

One marvelous Mallorca morning, I walked into a convenience store down the street from my hotel. I brought my stuff to the cash register and the man behind the counter was welcoming, asked me where I was from. Somehow we started talking about The Camino. He had gone to college in Burgos which is one of the cities I went to on The Camino. It has the 2nd largest cathedral in Spain and although I had decided I wasn't going to walk the entire Camino that was one of the places I made it a point to see for that reason. He told me that he worked with his cousin and if I ever wanted to stop by to feel free and we could have coffee and talk about traveling. I honestly don't know why I said I'd stop by the next day, but those are the words that came right on out of the lipsticked hole in my face.

His dark earth eyes had a sudden sparkle and the corners of his mouth slyly turned up. That evening I kept thinking about him. He was not my type per se but when I traveled it's like my whole world internally and externally opened up. It's not that he wasn't handsome. I am just usually attracted to white boys with blue eyes and beards or Latin men and he was of Indian decent. In my head I had made up this Spanish love affair and here on the island of Mallorca I met someone who was not Spanish. Ah, this is why as much as possible don't have expectations. Just be open to what the world offers you. So, I decided to!

After hot air ballooning, a glorious nap and sitting poolside while looking at the Mediterranean, I was still thinking about this guy. I said I'd come by, I wanted to see him again. Feeling like a teenager, nervous and excited, I gathered my courage to go to his store. When I arrived his face lit up. He was genuinely surprised and delighted to see me. He told me he thought I would come by earlier and that his cousin bet him I wouldn't show. His cousin had made plans for dinner and he was wondering if we could meet up a couple of hours later. I thought why not because I didn't have anything else going on.

When I came back we ended up eating Indian food in their back room that his cousin had brought. It was filled with warmth, hints of spice tickled my tongue, teasing and then melting away. I ate with my fingers and treasured every taste. After, we decided to walk by a park and monument area and on our way back he asked how old I thought he was, I said 30 or 33 and he said yes and kissed me on the lips. I was pleasantly surprised, both by his answer and the show of affection. I asked him to explain and he said that his birth certificate said he was 30 but he was actually 33, something about the government in India. I wasn't paying a lot of attention, a bit in awe by the kiss.

We were going to go out dancing. There were some pretty fancy clubs, but after all the fun we were having I just wanted to talk to him more. I in no uncertain terms said," You should come home with me," and he did. He came back to my hotel and I never realized just how privileged I was until he told me the amount he brought home working seven days a week, twelve hours a day for two weeks, was what I was spending on my hotel a night. It was such an eye opening experience for this middle class American woman. I wasn't born into money and the only reason I could afford the hotel was that I barely paid rent and had gotten my divorce settlement.

I didn't want to feel bad or guilty about it, but at first I did. I recognize that I was very lucky to be born white looking (I am mixed heritage with Mexican, Spanish, Scottish, Irish and more.) I present white and straight. I was also born and raised not only in the United States, but in Bay Area of California. All of this became crystal clear as we sat on the CA king bed.

We had brought some items from his store, had some wine and then we were naked. I had never had sex with someone of the Muslim religion and didn't know that they shower after they have sex. Needless to say, I was quite clean that evening and the next morning.

In the morning after he left I said I'd see him later, which I did, we walked by the harbor and said goodbye my last night there. I told him I needed to get up early and get a good night's sleep. He understood and we exchanged numbers to talk on-line using WhatsApp. The real reason I didn't want to spend the night with him was that after we were intimate, it dawned on me that ultimately I loved sex with women more. I decided it was time. I was ready to go back to women.

Barcelona Gay boys

Before leaving Mallorca, I looked on Airbnb to find a place to stay in Barcelona, the last part of my six week Spanish exploration. I came across these guys that called themselves Dementes Argentinians. They were gay artists and chefs studying in Barcelona originally from Argentina. The room was only $20euro a night and they sounded intriguing. Other people might think I was crazy, but something about them seemed fun.

On my arrival in Barcelona I stopped at a liquor store and bought a red Spanish wine as a gift for them. After walking up the very narrower three flights of stairs in the brick building with my back pack and the bottle of wine, I knocked on the door. When they answered and I presented the bottle, their faces lit up! I was in. I knew we were going to get alone swimmingly. They were a couple in their 20's and so adorable! One of them didn't speak much English and I not much Spanish, but we figured it out and smiled a lot at each other.

My room was the second on the left. There was a small hallway when you first entered. Their room was the first on the left and then after mine was another hallway leading to the only bathroom and two other bedrooms. After the bathroom was the kitchen and the large dining/living room area. One wall in the shared space was all windows. Their art was on the other walls in all different colors. They were actually painting on the wall of the long hallway in black light paint.

As they showed me to my room they let me know they didn't have sheets for my bed (but they would be getting them.) I figured they were in the wash or something. I hung out in the living room and chatted with another gay, demented Argentinian with thick dark glasses, a bountiful belly and kind eyes. He was another roommate. A few hours later my hosts were back and exclaimed, "We have your sheets!" and shook a plastic bag enthusiastically. They had just bought them! I thought to myself, "Hey at least I knew they are clean." They promptly put them on my bed and I took a nap before going out to my first dinner in Barcelona at 10:30pm.

The following night they made me a traditional Argentinian meal and invited friends to join. There were five of us and our conversations ranged from art to American politics to dating beautiful black men. We got drunk on lots of red Spanish wine, and they told me the places I had to see while I was in town. They told me about the Dali museum. It was a two hour train ride each way and I wasn't sure if I wanted to spend one of my days doing that. They insisted I make the trek.

I had no idea how big of a fan I was of the surrealist painter until I experienced what use to be his house turned into a museum. Unbeknownst to me, Dali had painted a fresco. The fresco was quite complicated. On one end of the room is the body of woman in a red dress. On the other end of the room is the body of a man in blue pants with a bare chest that is made of drawers. They are both reaching towards what I think is Dali's idea of heaven. I looked up so long trying to comprehend his genius, my neck hurt. I had to keep moving it down and then up again. That entire day I feasted my eyes on melting clocks, psychedelic colors and the idea that I was surrounded by and breathing in Greatness.

The outside of the museum was a castle with eggs on top. It was insane and amazing. That day ended up being one of the highlights of my six week trip. I would have never gone there if it hadn't been for the demented Argentinians. The generosity of time and spirit of humans that have welcomed me into their homes and lives are the real souvenirs I brought home from my adventures.

Barcelona Clothing Store

I loved collecting purses and wanted one to remember Barcelona. I had spent an inspiring morning at the Sagrada Familia and on my way back to my apartment I wandered into a purse store. I fell in love with a purse. It had brightly colored embroidered flowers, but the cherry on top was the inside. The lining was a royal purple with a print that had "sex, love fun for everyone," printed all over. I had to get that purse but it was not cheap. I decided to google the brand Desigual. There was a store only 2 metro stops away! So I hopped on the metro and as I came up from underground it started pouring down rain. I looked around to see the store and in bright letters like a beacon of sunshine and beautiful purse hope, there it was Desigual!

I ran as to not get entirely soaked and when I entered the store, I was instantly enveloped in the perky hues of jewel toned fabrics. I was in a giant clothing hug. I yearned to touch every dress, feel the smooth material against my skin as my eyes swallowed the many shapes and designs. I was in shopping bliss. For the first time there were gorgeous garments, every one of which fit when I tried it on. I must have tried on over twenty dresses, skirts and tops, then shoes!

I found the exact purse and standing in the dressing room I felt like a model. I was radiant in the deep shades of rubies, topaz, emerald and onyx mixed print dresses. I wanted to buy them all but settled on one dress, one purse and the most gorgeous shoes I had ever laid eyes on. They were high platform sandals. The heels were a tan color but the shoes had circle swirls of teal, raspberry, orange and purple. I sat there with them on my feet and knew it was impractical. When would I really wear them? But how could I not bring them home with me?

I began to have anxiety about the money for all of it, if I purchased all three items it would be over $200. I sat there and thought: is this me or the voice of my ex that we can't spend money. Reminding myself that I was in charge of my money now and that I didn't need permission, I decided to buy the three items. The sense of personal power was profound and I let all of the guilt about spending money slide off me like the raindrops outside. I walked out of that Barcelona store proud and full of glee.

The following night I took myself to the opera wearing all three treasures on the night that would have been my 14th wedding anniversary. Watching a three hours German tragedy in Spain was not at all what I had envisioned for that day in May. The most ironic part was that after all the walking I had done on The Camino without one blister, walking half a mile in my new heels I gave myself three! Oh, life, you have such a sense of humor.

How Much Could I do in One Barcelona Day?

I woke up in my apartment and had no idea how much I would explore, taste, see, and involve myself in that day. I took a bus to the area where the Picasso museum was. Before I started searching for the museum, I had breakfast at an out-side café. I had not had churros and chocolate and thought it was appropriate because I was going to the Chocolate mu-seum after the Picasso museum. I not only had the churros and chocolate but a coffee drink and a ham and cheese sand-wich. The chocolate that you dip the churros in is basically hot chocolate pudding, it's so rich and ridiculously delicious. I ran out of churros and wasn't sure if I should, but I drank most of the remaining brown velvet liquid. It was one of the best things I had ever tasted.

I then walked way past the Picasso museum and finally

found it. I didn't realize how diverse Picasso's work was. It was breathtaking. I loved the pieces that were parts of larger paintings and after seeing all of the individual paintings to see them all together for a masterpiece. Mind boggling to see all the genius, madness magic on canvas.

After attempting to take in all of that, I found my way to the Chocolate museum. A fun thing about the *Museo de Xocolot* was that your ticket was a chocolate bar! It was a kick to see so many things made out of chocolate. There was the giant Gaudi lizard, the Sagrada Familia replica (the most amazing building I have ever been in but that is another story), Michelangelo's "La Pieta" and many other chocolate creations.

After leaving the *Museo de Xocolot,* I took the metro to attend a paella and sangria making class. I finally found the bar we were supposed to meet in and thinking I was late, discovered I was the first one there. The Spanish have a different sense of time. I fit right in, must be my heritage, I laughed to myself. The second to arrive were these two guys in their early twenties. One was blond with a happy face like a cherub, the other was taller with dark hair, and a goatee. We instantly hit it off and I quickly figured out they were a couple; yay more gay guy friends in Barcelona! We talked a little before others arrived and I found out their names were Gus and Russ, adorable! They were also Americans recently graduating from a school in Boston and had been traveling through Europe for over one month.

Pretty soon others arrived along with our teacher and guide. We all walked to the market to get the ingredients we would be using to cook the paella and to make the sangria. This was the most eye-candy filled market I had ever been in. There were such gorgeous displays of fruit, including dragon fruit which I had never even heard of. It was a dark pink on the outside and white with little black seeds on the inside. There were stands with freshly made juices, stunning spices, including a whole area with just flavored salts! I was compelled to buy raspberry salt, it was bright pink! There was candy, vegetables, fish, meat, you name it! If it's edible and attractive it was there. We were all so taken with our surroundings, our guide had to keep us focused as he bought all of our dinner and drink fixings.

Once we were able to tear our eyes away from all the yumminess, we headed to the kitchen. As part of the class I helped chop vegetables and even got a picture stirring paella in the giant pan. It must have been at least four feet wide! While the paella was cooking we added the fruit and red wine together to create the sangria. There was another alcohol added that made it quite a strong but delicious beverage.

After everything was made, the guys and I sat at a table with a mom and daughter, also Americans. During dinner the daughter invited us all to go on a pub crawl. At first I thought, "Labris, you are 39 years old, what are you thinking going on a pub crawl? You've never been on a pub crawl!" Luckily, I didn't listen to that voice and instead thought, "Why not, when would I be in Barcelona again?"

We ended up meeting at a student hostel for the crawl. We were told not to call it that and instead we were, "celebrating someone's birthday." There were around fifteen of us and the first bar we went to served the best shots I had ever tasted in my life. Being a woman who had cherished some liquor in her life, that was saying something.

The first shot was some sort of citrus vodka, set on fire, drunk from its sugared rim and finished with a slice of orange whose bursting tang soothed my steaming tongue. The next was, to this day, my all-time favorite. The bartender lit up a line of alcohol on the bar and we roasted marshmallows. We then dipped the marshmallows into our shot, drank it then ate the marshmallow. The smoky, buttery sweetness swayed from taste bud to taste bud. The third shot I think I just inhaled pure grass green alcohol from a straw. I'm still not sure about that one but I do have pictures to prove it!

The next bar on the list; there were several; I decided to flirt subtly with a friend of the guys that were hosting the pub crawl. I know that I previously said I was going back to women. My sexuality confused even me at that point in my life. Also, drunk Labris was different then sober Labris. At that point in the evening I was certainly not sober and the young Belgium man had peaked my interest.

I stole his vodka and cranberry, one of my favorite drinks even though it took four or five sips to figure out what drink it was. His name was Thomas and I liked his lankiness, short blond hair and honey eyes. He and I started talking about Spain, travel and then he lightheartedly made fun of me for being an American. Speaking about America, he mentioned being a sports writer and that he should have been at the Indie500 as he had covered it the last three years. I asked if he liked to drive fast and he answered that he didn't have a driver's license. I told him that was ok and that I didn't get mine until I was 28. His response was, "Yea, I'll have mine by then."

In my head I was thinking, by then? What? How old is he, more importantly, how much younger is he then me, and how drunk am!? I later found out he was somewhere between 24-26, he never told me exactly. We continued our banter past when everyone I knew had left. I decided to stay for one more drink with the hosts and Thomas. The drink was fruity and bright pink with some kind of rum, the specialty cocktail of the night.

Thomas invited me back to his place with his roommates but I was not interested in that nonsense. Hanging out in a stinky boy flat filled with strangers, no gracias. He walked me towards the area where taxis were and throwing caution to the wind I wrote my Spanish phone number down and asked him if he'd like to meet for coffee sometime.

He was quiet, then all of a sudden he stopped, turned towards me, put his hands on my face and kissed me up against a stone wall. It felt like a dream or scene in a romcom. We started making out in the middle of the sidewalk, in Barcelona at 1am. After we came up for air he asked me what I wanted. My answer: "You should come home with me." And he did. I tried that line twice and both times it worked. It's a good line. I recommend it, but you need to say it with conviction. With that decided we grabbed a cab. His hands were all over me in the backseat. He told me how excited he was to be with an older woman who wasn't afraid to say what she wanted. He was tired of fucking 20 year olds. I reassured him I was definitely not 20 and yes, I would tell him what I wanted.

At my apartment, in bed we were both too drunk. He confessed that nothing was going on down there because of alcohol. I didn't mind, I liked his honesty and carefree attitude. We laid there, exposed, exploring each other's unfamiliar bodies, while the dim light peeked through from the kitchen. His lips, two inviting creatures, played hide and go seek with mine. He held me all night and would wake up randomly to kiss me passionately and then fall back to sleep. His arms and legs like vines around me. As the hours of night turned to day I was reminded of one more example of what I didn't even know I had been missing in my marriage. I hadn't been kissed and held all night by someone in far too long. Jay had stopped holding me like that years before. So, I half slept encircled by the cloud white body of an inebriated young man until the rude awakenings of the morning decided to remind us of our alcohol consumption.

The night before we had made plans about how we were going to have sex every day until the moment I had to leave. That was not meant to be. He left and I never saw him again. I was disappointed at first but came to the conclusion that I didn't travel to Barcelona to stay in bed the whole time, some of the time, most definitely, but not the whole time. Things happen for a reason and the amount of sightseeing and self-discovery I had over that week was attained due to my adventurous ways outside, not inside, the bedroom.

Sagrada Familia

The following day, no more hangover, I hopped on the Metro to go to the place I had built up so much anticipation to see. The exit was even called *Sagrada Familia*. The basilica was Gaudi's greatest work and was still being completed. It was the one structure of his I had not yet seen. The whole reason I was drawn to Barcelona was Gaudi's unique architecture.

When I came out of the metro into the afternoon sun, the giant pillars were the first thing I noticed. My eyes gazed upon its grace and enormity. The more I stared the more the details began to immerge. The basilica took up an entire city block all the way around. Behind scaffolding were groups of different colored balls that glittered in the sunlight. What looked like apples and oranges all stacked together had been built on top of some of the pillars. This man was not only an artist but a mastermind.

The building felt alive. My neck strained as I continued to stare up at it while I waited in line. I would have waited all day for even a minute inside. I could hardly stand it, the day had finally arrived. The moment was coming when I'd get to go inside. Being in the same vicinity was an experience I could never have imagined. When I entered the *Sagrada Familia*, I was encased in the structure where he had created the divine. Tears rolled down both of my cheeks. I had never been in such a spectacular space created by humans. I stood there under the pillars that were made to resemble trees hundreds of feet high. I felt my spirit spread with their roots and up through their ceiling branches. I soaked in their Grace. I am not a religious person but at that moment, breathing it all in, I was in the presence of what many call God.

I have been in churches in my life, several on the Camino, but this was in a realm all its own. I actually kneeled down and prayed in one of the pews. The last time I did that I was a little girl in the 1980's in a Catholic Church in Berkeley with my grandmother Mary, "Grams" is what I called her. Kneeling at that Spanish alter I knew my Grams was with me. She was the woman who would pick me up from school and buy me an ice cream cone, who told me I could be anything I wanted in this world. Grams was my favorite parent who earned her high school diploma at the age of 75. She died on her own terms at the age of 93. Feeling the magnitude of the columns, witnessing the bright colors of stained glass and hearing the echoing music of the organ, it was all her. She wrapped me up in her giant love that defied death.

16

Dee –The Most Romantic Friend I Never Dated

If you're wondering who I had the feelings for, it was an excellent love affair, with no sex involved. You might have an eyebrow raised, but just wait.

I met her years prior when I was still somewhat happily married. I had joined several local groups to get my interior design business going. I was at a women's breakfast one morning and had to leave the meeting early to get to work. I was walking to my car and heard someone running behind me. I felt a tap on my shoulder and this beautiful woman with short dark blond hair and sparkly emerald eyes said, "Hi, I'm Dee and I wanted to introduce myself to you before you left." I was very much taken aback, but flattered. She told me she worked for a solar company and I thought we might be able to network. We exchanged cards and I went to work.

That same night, I went to another networking event and she was there! We started talking and I began to feel like she was flirting with me. I liked it, which freaked me out. At some point I said to her, "I have to go home to my wife."

I didn't see her again until 3 months after I left my marriage. It was Pink Saturday, the first Saturday in June for Gay Pride in Santa Cruz. I didn't know anyone else that was going, I just felt that I needed to be there. It might sound strange, but every once in a long while I get these messages in my gut that tell me to do something. I have learned to listen. Something good if not fantastic happens as a result.

I arrived at the museum, where they were hosting the Pink Saturday party. After being there about five minutes, I saw a woman that looked familiar. She greeted me with her beautiful smile and I recognized that it was Dee. We introduced ourselves again and then ended up spending the entire night dancing (even on the stage!) When the museum party was winding down we went to a nearby club with her friends.

At one point we were dirty dancing and I mentioned that my feet hurt and I was going to take off my shoes. She dragged me off the dance floor, took my shoes off and began rubbing my feet in the middle of the busy walk area to get to the dance floor! I felt like Cinderella! I honestly was a little embarrassed but also adored it because I had never had anyone do anything like that.

After a couple of minutes we went back to the dance floor. At this point it was nearing 1am. As we're dancing she casually mentioned her girlfriend. She said she was in Virginia for three months at a vegan ashram learning how to become a chef. I was a bit confused but mostly bummed because I thought by her behavior that she was single and had hoped for more than a friendship.

We began contacting each other daily and making plans to hang out. Our first evening, she took me on a picnic, with the basket, homemade snacks and everything. We sat talking back and forth overlooking the ocean in shades of lavender and turquoise as the sun set around us.

She got me to do things I would never previously dared to do. We rode a rollercoaster over and over on a Wednesday night after eating deep fried Oreos. We snuck on to someone's small raft in the harbor and watched the moon's light shine on the feathers of a sleeping pelican. We ate french fries at midnight and walked through caves at the beach.

Dee was the first person to really get me after my marriage ended. I was starved for attention and for someone to love me as I was. She was the first woman after my ex-wife to pay attention to me. What I mean by attention, it was obvious that when we were together, all of her focus was on me. She kept her phone on silent and we spent hours talking and laughing.

Her face would light up when she would see me. Her genuineness drew me to her. Dee and I could have been in a giant paper bag and we would have had fun in it. She'd have noticed the color variations in the paper and I'd have commented on the toasty tree smell. We'd both have laughed and skipped around in it. It was the carefree beauty of us that I cherished.

Through the years we became even closer, like best friends. She was a different kind of best friend, though. A BFF that flirts with you, spends the night in your bed (nothing sexual) and rubs your feet while you're watching a movie. It was hard to keep my feelings at bay. I tried to kiss her one night and she turned away. She didn't want to complicate our friendship and that she didn't feel that way about me.

So what did I do with all of the memories, feelings and

emotions? Did I vilify her? Did I push her away and pretend our friendship never existed? I wanted to at first, but that was my bruised ego. Instead, I took some time to reflect on our friendship and how important she was to me. Looking back, her attention was what I needed right after my break up. Not having the complication of sex, exclusivity and all the couple relationship boundaries was not what I needed from her.

She was always my cheerleader. She encouraged me to go for whatever dream I wanted to pursue. She was the one that I first told about wanting to write this book. Writing a book was a secret I had kept to myself for months. One night, with hot tea in our hands, I confessed it to her. She was so excited about the idea. Then, she remembered she had taken a number off of a flyer for a book completion group. She gave me the number and the next day I called and signed up for the next session of classes.

I wasn't about to throw so much friend love out the window because of unrequited romantic love. I forgave both us for the complicated and mixed signals. I allowed myself to know that we were meant to be wonderfully close platonic friends. We are still close today and her face still lights up when she sees me.

17

Self-Discovery Through Art and Adrenaline

Besides listening to music and being supported by the people around me, putting my energy toward creating art was another important way I worked through my unhappiness. I created bright abstract flowers using pastels with my fingers. I would tune out the whole world. I'd get lost in the magenta, lime and tangerine chalk smeared on the paper. I somehow managed to get it in my hair and up my forearm. Some of my brightest works came from inner melancholy and anger. When I was physically unable to cry, the royal purple and crimson would soar across my sheet and turn into petals reaching to the edges. I didn't have to explain myself. I blended colors so my mind and spirit could be content in the moment. I was even proud of some of what I created. I originally did them for myself and then decided to show close friends. I was hesitant in case they were crap. My friends loved how cheerful they were and encouraged me to have an art show.

I was trying to network in the LGBT community and found an open house at the local Adult Store. One of the owners, Sharon, identified as part of the queer community and I thought it'd be fun to see the shop. Who doesn't like an excuse to check out a sex shop?! The meeting in all honesty was a bust, except that I told Sharon about my art and she said I should stop by sometime with samples. I tried to act casual but was doing somersaults inside.

A couple of weeks later I met Sharon at her store. I brought along some smaller sized pastels and cards with pictures I had taken of the pastels and flowers in nature. She looked at the vibrant canary, raspberry and cobalt pastels and said that they were different then what was usually featured. I thought that was a nice rejection, but it wasn't! Sharon said it would be refreshing to have my art up. I was elated! My first art show at a sex shop, so perfect. This was a sign I was on the correct path. The shop was part of First Fridays in downtown Santa Cruz. The First Friday events were held every month and local artists showcased their art at different venues. Sharon said my art could stay up the entire month of October.

A very good friend and fellow artist made frames for me out of drift and barn wood. We thought the rustic look of the wood was a wonderful complement to the energetic pastels. He help me hang all of my pieces, a total of twenty, including some photos that were printed on metal. The white walls were covered in vivacious 24"x36" pastel petals.

I was so nervous and excited. Most of my friends came, even some coworkers. It was such a fun and silly night. The store put out wine, crackers and cheeses. I couldn't help myself and bought bite sized cupcakes with frosting flowers in orange and dark pink. Watching my friends look at the sex toys, giggle and purchase who knows what, was one of my favorite nights. I hadn't felt that full of happiness in a very long time. And the cherry on top, I even sold some art!

Diving into my 37th year

My birthday was on a Friday. I took half a day off work and didn't tell a soul. What I was going to do. I had fantasized about it for years but Jay would never have allowed it; the cost or trepidation or who knows what excuse. I think the main reason I was there was to not only prove to myself I could do this but that I could do anything and needed permission from no one to live my life.

When I entered the industrial building, I was immediately enveloped in testosterone. There was only one other woman there, at least 10 years my junior. She was the receptionist and quite friendly when I walked up to the desk. She asked if I wanted pictures, or a video, or both of the experience. I wanted it all, including the black t-shirt. I gave her my credit card and she handed me a piece of paper. I sat down to read. At the bottom of the sheet I was required to print and then sign the words: this could result in my physical injury or death. I took a deep breath and feeling 90% confident that I wasn't going to die on my birthday, signed and dated it. Yes, my 37th birthday seemed like the perfect day to jump out of an airplane.

After I returned the release form, I sat there looking at all the boys. I guess legally they were men, but their energy was so playful. They were adrenaline junkies to the T; jumping around, giving each other high fives and comparing jump stories. I thought to myself, am I seriously putting my life into the hands of one of these 22 year olds? The answer: yep!

I sat there patiently waiting and noticed a really macho guy in the group. As he walked towards me, I wished, "anyone but him, anyone but him." Luckily, the birthday gods were on my side and he walked right past me to two guys that were there for one of their birthdays. The next guy came right up to me with his tooth filled smile and kind praline eyes. He introduced himself as Max. He asked if I had come by myself and was impressed when I answered that I had. He then looked down at my feet and saw that I was wearing four inch cork heeled sandals and asked, "You're not wearing those, right?" I laughed and said no, because I had heard that I could land barefoot on the beach. He started telling me about the process. We put on gear and then walked outside into the glorious sunlight to wait for the plane. He took a video of me asking my information and why I had chosen to skydive. I don't remember what words came out, but inside I thought, "If I can survive leaving my wife, I can survive anything." He told me he would be taking pictures and some video throughout the experience.

Another young man joined us who was coming along because he needed more jumps for his certification. They started talking about their experiences and Max said he had jumped from planes all around the world. He said all of them were great except when he hit the side of the plane jumping out of one in Sweden. "Holy shit!" I thought, how did he manage that? Fortunately, at this point the plane arrived. I am using the term "plane" loosely here: it looked like the size of my mini cooper. But, I was committed and at this point not even nervous.

I hopped in with the guys and as I looked around the plane it looked like the inside was made of aluminum foil held together with duct tape. I was still ok with this and when the pilot asked how far up I wanted to go, 8,000, 10,000 or 14,000 feet, I said 14,000, why not? I didn't think I'd be doing this again anytime soon so why not go as high as possible.

So, there I was in an aluminum foil airplane attached to 120lb Max who I had freely entrusted with my life to jump out of a plane over the ocean at 14,000 feet on my 37th birthday. The plane kept going up and up. The other guy jumped out at 10,000 feet and I was still fine. I was fine the entire rest of the way up until the moment Max told me we were going to scoot our way toward the door of the plane and then dangle our legs. At that point my inner voice was like, "No, I'm good, no scooting necessary, there's no need to dangle my legs, I'm just fine right here." But, my inner voice had no say as my body was attached to Max who was scooting toward the ever closer opening of blue sky and sun.

I remember feeling my heart racing all the way down to my dangling feet. Then, I was looking back up at the plane. I was doing it. The words, "I'm not going to die, I'm not going to die, I'm not going to die," kept rushing through my head as I plummeted toward the Pacific Ocean. Earlier he told me to scream on the way down because you have to breathe to scream. Breathing was a good thing, when I could. The air felt violent as I sped through it and I attempted to scream but don't know if sound came out. I was falling in chaos. Everything felt frenzied and then the shoot opened. I could really breathe. I was soaring in the midafternoon sun over the Pacific Ocean, looking down on the coastline of the Central Coast of California.

Gorgeous doesn't begin to describe the view. I felt like I was in someone else's beautiful dream. He started swaying us left to right and I quickly was aware of my stomach and that I didn't want to lose my breakfast all over us and on video. I politely yelled if he could stop the swaying. My face might have also been the color of fireplace ashes, so he stopped immediately.

My body calmed and I didn't want the ride to end. Up there, I had no responsibilities, pain or brokenness. I was brave and free. As the beach grew closer, I tried to hold on to those feelings as I lifted my legs up and then landed in a running fall. I had done it. Happy birthday to me.

18

FRIENDS and Tattoos – these are two of my Favorite Things

I spoke with my birthday buddy, (her birthday is the day before mine and I remind here that she's older even if it's just for a day) her and I are very similar and I know she won't judge me. I'm not saying my other friend's do, they so don't. Jules just gets it! She's divorced, but she has two fantastic kids and I chose not to have children. She has also had someone cheat on her. We both found out within three months of each other that we had been cheated on. We both are silly, sometimes obsessive and liked talking to each other about our sexual exploits. I called her because I had started seeing a 30 year old with midday sky blue eyes and a light brown beard. Yes I have a type of men, who knew, certainly not me. Although Jay did have the ocean blue eyes going on. I digress, so I called Jules because I was upset that this guy that I just met had been texting me but can't see me until next week. My housemate is returning home from being gone three months and I felt uncomfortable having him here right after she would return home. Jules was great, she nailed it, I feel uncomfortable having him here, but I enjoy him and don't want him to go away so I was going to compromise my comfortability for him. Such nonsense I put myself through! He owns his own home so why can't we go there? It's this whole thing of wanting to please others first. Both Jules and I had narcissistic mothers and grew up knowing it was never about us. She understood my behavior of feeling responsible for someone else's feelings, making them more important than my feelings. She also understood doing it and then being resentful and irritated at the other person.

The other important thing that we shared (unfortunately) was that we both dated the exes that cheated on us. We were in different situations but when you have been cheated on there is a certain feeling that you don't fully grasp if it hasn't happened to you. The idea that we also both were working on forgiveness and reconciliation, I felt was rare to be happening at the same time. We didn't feel comfortable to share with other friends as we knew it probably wasn't the best idea to be with the cheaters, but it was something we each had to do. Neither of us was needing to feel or hear other people's judgement on what we were doing. Ultimately, we figured out that we couldn't get back together with them. I was sorry that we both had to go through it but it was also comforting to know at least we had one another.

With all of the internal struggling and reinventing I was doing, the one constant was being surrounded by supportive friends and family. There had been countless hours of compassionate ears listening and hearts accepting me in all of my brokenness. I couldn't have done it alone. In all of my adventures I am never alone, I have the love of my closest people with me always.

Tattooed with a college friend

I had been wanting a tattoo to signify my new life, something that would represent who I was; single, mostly carefree and turning another year older. I liked to think of her as my alter-ego but the people closest to me knew she was me in tattooed form. I knew I wanted to have a dancing woman, with wings. I had many ideas and wings was something that kept coming up. At one point I pictured my entire back covered with them. I decided that I didn't have to be so literal: the wings are a given, my soul having no confines. I also knew I wanted the tattoo on my left thigh. Years ago, in 1998 when I was 22 right before my 23rd birthday I got a tattoo on my right arm. I felt balanced with having one on my right upper arm and the other on my upper left thigh. Not only did I want my tattoo to be a winged dancing lady but I loved the idea of my tattoo having a tattoo. I am a Taurus and relate to my astrological sign quite a bit. I felt that symbol would be a perfect tattoo for "her." I told Jack, the adorable 28 year old fully tattooed tattoo artist everything including that I wanted "her" to be wearing a corset and a skirt with high heels and makeup. I desired a representation of feminine strength. When he first showed me the drawing it was on tracing paper and was huge, I figured it was to show me the details. When I asked him the size, he pointed to the paper. The dancing winged woman was almost the length of my entire thigh, but I fell in love with her instantly. He had added musical notes and that gave her even more life in my eyes.

My first session with the outline and shading, was with my friend Di. I had known her since my UCSC days in the late 90's. Di's birthday was also in April and we decided to both get tattoos. She was visiting from Fresno for our second annual birthday celebration in San Francisco. We had lost track of one another somewhere in the middle of my marriage. I had made the mistake of telling my wife that I had once been attracted to her and even though Di was in our wedding party and I was in Di's wedding to her wife, Jay never liked her.

I'm trying to not judge myself too harshly on giving up my friendship with Di for my wife, we do things we are not proud of sometimes in the name of love and that was one of a few. I also gave up my best friend, Sara, from high school. I rationalized it to myself somehow. Years later we luckily reconnected and forgave each other and ourselves for our rash 20 something year old selves. I digress!

The interesting part of reconnecting with Di was that within a month after I left Jay and was living in my studio I received a message from her on Facebook. I had not heard from her in over 5 years and the message was actually sent 3 days after I had left Jay. The Universe works in mysterious ways. Di and I ended up pretty much right where we had left off. She was so kind to me and listened to my tales of woe and heart ache. I appreciated her sentiments that my ex was an idiot and would never meet anyone as wonderful as me. It is good to have all kinds of friends: the ones that are fair and impartial, can see all kinds of views and the ones that are 100% on your side that tell you that your ex is just wrong. Di was the latter, which I cherished. She was one of my champions.

Back to the tattoo parlor, Di's tattoo was the Aries symbol to represent her and her daughter's astrological sign and bond. I teased her while we were there because Di was very butch, and her tattoo was about three inches around where mine was at least eight. She went first and was good natured about my jesting. I was so grateful to have her there to distract me because when it was my turn, I got to lie down but my thigh hurt like a pissed off demon was in that needle! Good god that was painful! I don't know why I didn't think it would hurt that much. I am convinced that when you are 22 you just don't feel pain as much as when you're almost 40. Also, this tattoo was not on my arm and was considerably larger. We ended up being there for around three hours and then were rushed because we had tickets for a concert in San Francisco that night. Why I thought getting a tattoo on my thigh on the same day I was planning on dancing all night was a good idea, was beyond me. I can't believe some of the things I did in the first years after I left my marriage, but damn I had a hell of a lot of fun.

19

The Older Butch

I had met her thirteen years prior, when I was married. I was intimidated by her presence, intellect, sexuality, age and the ultimate kicker, eyes that were the color of a river on a hot summer's day. I met her again a couple of years after my marriage ended. Our meeting was under the guise of volunteering on a 40 year celebration memory book. It was for the health center I used to work at and she was a member the board of directors. Glyn and I met several times at her house to work on the project. She asked me for a hike. I invited her to my art show at a flower shop.

After she stopped by my art show, she invited over for dinner. On the table were six individual flowers put in their own vases. She explained that she was inspired by my art. She was smooth. She had cooked grass fed New York steaks and organic asparagus. I contributed my dark chocolate brownies with special chocolate and caramel pieces I added for her. She sent me home with oat cakes she had baked early, one especially for me. We talked about our exes, travel, the project, ice cream.

I had her over next. I made her a bacon and mushroom

frittata and I didn't bake early on a Saturday for just anyone. I wore an apron in a flirty 50's sexy housewife way. She asked if we could date after the project, she was nervous and fidgety. Gleefully, I interrupted, "Yes, yes, yes!" She was shy about kissing me because I worked for a dentist. She said she felt she needed to have mouth wash so she wanted to wait. Yes, she was quirky, among other things.

The next day, when I arrived at her house, she ran up to my car. She showed me the piece of gum that was in her mouth and then her head was in my open window, lips on mine in a haze of excitement. After the kiss I didn't know what to do and she reminded me, "Turn off your car." I felt crazy, couldn't sleep or eat, who was she, did she really like me? She adored me and I her and I tried to find ways to push her away, she was too old for me, too settled, she was a Leo on the cusp of Virgo, anything, anything I could think of to make this go away because I was petrified of being broken again. She was the only woman since Jay that had adored me, wanted me, the inside me, not the size DD, blonde haired me.

I wanted to relax about all of it, exhale for once and not worry about another woman breaking my barely mended heart. I wanted to, but I couldn't. We had a date, so I went to her house for dinner. She had bought a bottle of champagne called, "The Lady of Spain," she looked at me with a giant grin and said, "Do you get it," of course I did. She was so thoughtful. She knew how important the Camino adventure had been for me. Why did I feel undeserving? Why did I question her? Why was it so incredibly difficult for me to believe that she could care this much for me? Maybe because the woman that I thought I would grow old loving, the one that I held every night since I was 23 betrayed me by falling for another? Was that why? Was that why I didn't trust the kindness? If Jay couldn't treat me this way after loving me for over a decade, buying a house and trying to have a baby, why should she?

I answered my own question: because this dark haired, super sexy, butch, 20 years older than me woman named Glyn was not my ex-wife. Glyn was a new crush filled with so much light and strength, so much confidence, openness and intrigue. She was the first to treat me this way in so many, many years. The rest wanted me for my body and my mind and soul were just okay. The body was number one and the rest was well, the rest. She had not had my body and yet it seemed desired all of me.

I had all this weirdness around what other people would think of our 20 year age difference. I also told myself that I was so independent, I didn't need a lover and when in a relationship I become so into the person. I wanted to spend all my time with them.

I needed to find a healthy balance. Luckily Glyn and I had different schedules so I couldn't lose myself in her. I physically, emotionally and spiritually could not have treasured someone else over the first few years after my marriage. My heart was shattered. Or to put it more exactly: my ex-wife ripped out my heart, threw it on the cold cement, stomped on it hard with her men's size 10 1/2s and then left it there to die. That's how my heart felt. But I picked it up, cleaned it and brought it back from the brink of death. I loved myself back to full life. My heart still had a couple of bruises and a few scratches but it was again, a complete, full loving heart.

I was a cross between tenuous and running away screaming from this developing affection between Glyn and myself. I didn't know where she fit in to my adventurer, world travelling lifestyle or if I wanted her to.

I began to realize I wasn't exaggerating the age difference. It was an issue. We didn't have much in common when we stopped working on the project. The best thing about our relationship was the captivating sex. She asked me to be her girlfriend and I asked what that meant to her, even though I knew very much what she meant. She said that we would be exclusive sexually. I immediately shut down. The idea of not having sex with anyone else made me instantly want to be able to. That was a sign. I am a monogamous person when I am in love. I can appreciate attractive people, but I have no desire to be with anyone except who I am crazy about. She wanted much more than I could give her. I wished that I could feel the way she felt about me but when you don't feel it, you don't feel it. She would have given me the world in a gold dipped bowl if I had asked for it. But she needed something in return, my heart, which I was not able to give.

She had left her strap at my house. How awkward was that? Here's the dick you fucked me with last week but I don't want to see you anymore. How would that not be a painful exchange? We sat on her porch and she was filled with grace and understanding. She asked if I wore the apron out of necessity or to be flirty, I told her both. She answered, "When you find someone who can have both parts of you, the devoted wife and the sex kitten, they are going to be the luckiest person." I started to cry. I knew what she meant. I hoped that someday I would find that person again.

Before I left that October night, she told me that she would be fine with being as she called it, "friends with benefits and appetizers." Food and sex were what we did fantastic together. The sex with her was all passion; hair pulling, spanking, everything with ferocity. I was tempted by her offer. I left and told her I'd keep it in mind, but I just couldn't go there with her then. A part of me thought she couldn't handle hanging out with me occasionally and that I had better just steer clear. She said she would leave it up to me to communicate with her. I waited a couple of weeks and thought about it. She was a grown woman and if she couldn't handle something she could let me know. Yes, I craved the sex with her.

One Friday night I called her from my car and left a message. I pondered, should I 1. Just hang up, 2. Only ask her to call me with no details or 3. Leave details. I went for option 3 because life can be so awesome when you go directly after what you desire. My message went something like this: "Hi Glyn, this is Labris, this is an official booty call in case you were wondering. I am calling you to come over tonight or sometime soon. Give me a call back if you're interested." About five minutes later her name appeared on my cell phone. She had liked the message and said she saved it to listen to if she ever had a bad day in the future. She asked if I was the same; still sexy, sweet and beautiful. I didn't know how to answer. So with a smile and a giggle I said I had not changed. Her response was, "yes, I'm interested!"

She showed up with many accoutrements, one of the best parts about our sex life together. After catching up in the living room we went right for the bed. I had half-jokingly asked her to bring some candles as a "punishment," for me. Low and behold in her bag of tricks was a brand new white taper. I know this might sound not very wild to some of you but it was the first time I had done anything that "daring" in the bedroom with a woman. The hot wax was such a turn on. Maybe I was a freak and if I so, I didn't care because I believe that this life of mine was meant for all kinds of experiences. So, the candle play lasted who knows how long because time flies when you are having fun. There is something about the juxtaposition of tenderness outside of the bedroom with the hard core passion inside the bedroom that was such a turn-on for me. We were up for hours and the morning sex was just as hot (ok not literally!) but just as passionate. We made pancakes and bacon together, cheered with orange juice and then she went home.

The next time we saw each other she had a surprise for me. I usually rejoiced in the idea of surprises but being that we were now doing this "Friends with Benefits and Appetizers," I hoped she hadn't gotten carried away. I was in the process of not feeling responsible for other people's feelings, extremely challenging, but I did my best to just go with it. As I sat across from her dark brown buzz cut, she asked if I would stay the night. I was luckily in the middle of a fork full of corned beef and cabbage because I needed a minute for my response. She had never asked me to stay the night at her place because she was worried about her 90 year old father in the next room. I thought, he was 90 for god's sake. He went to bed at 7pm and was hard of hearing, what was he going to know? But, I respected her boundaries and never pressed the issue.

In all honesty, I had not been a fan of sharing a bed with anyone all night. The theory of cuddly and spooning intrigued me but after about 20 minutes with whoever it was I thought, "Oh shit, what the hell have I gotten myself into? How long do I have to do this," or worse, "when can I kick them out?" I appreciated the men that only stayed a couple of hours. Some people might ask, "Did that make you feel used, not spending the night with someone, only having sex with them?" My answer, "Not at all. It was fantastic! I got the best of both worlds, all the pleasure and the whole bed to myself!"

So when being confronted with this all night option I wondered just how long I could reasonably take to chew this already soft bite of food. I slowly swallowed, smiled and politely said, "Oh, but what about your father?" She said that everything was taken care of. Well hell! But she had such a look of excitement and anticipation, and the sex with her was the kinkiest and hottest I had ever had, so I succumbed.

When we arrived at her house, we went straight to the garage. I knew the area well, that's where we worked on the volunteer project together. Were we going to sleep in her garage on a rainy January night? She had me close my eyes and open them when we were inside. My concern that she had gotten carried away was soon reality taken to the Nth degree. As my pupils took in the scene, I caught my breath as my jaw dropped; she had built a wooden 4 poster bed structure in one whole section of her garage. She had brought her bed from her house and enclosed it in this structure with dark sheer fabric curtains! If that wasn't over the top enough, she had garnet colored sheets on the queen sized mattress, lit midnight black candles, soul music going on her record player and extra blankets because it was cold.

In all of my years living and over half of those as a sexual adult, no one had ever built a structure so they could sleep/ have sex with me. So, in that situation I felt honored and guilty. We were not girlfriends. I was in it for the fantastic sex and didn't know how to react. I'm sure she saw my look of shock, even in the dimly lit room. I did smile because it really was unbelievable. I could only say. "Wow," and thanked her immensely for all of her time, effort and thoughtfulness. I couldn't let all of this actually seep in so I quickly started calling it the love den and said we should try it out. It was more of a sex den really because it was filled with pleasures of flesh not heart.

I only slept over once because it was winter and freezing even with the flannel sheets and blankets. Glyn treated me better than anyone, up until that point. All the men I had dated were just for sex. I wasn't ready for anything serious. She was definitely the best sex out of all the guys. I knew I would end up with a butch woman one day, just not her.

I was the most explorative with her and the last time we were naked together I asked her to bring over a blind fold and more candles. We had my place to ourselves. We skipped appetizers and went directly to my room for the benefits.

Thrown on my bed wearing my strapless black ribbed corset with fishnets and heels I asked her to take it all off me.

She had brought a riding crop that she'd told me about but we'd never played with. She turned me over and I felt a sting on my upper thigh, it moved to my ass and I told her it hurt. She called me a baby and I scowled at her. It was all in good, sexy fun. She moved on to another spot and it's sexy but I was confused about my feelings for it. We rolled around on my double bed and she started to take off my shoes. She struggled with the buckle and I told her she could just slip them off. She turned to me and said, "Are you telling me what to do." I replied, "Yes, I'm bossy." "A bossy bottom, nobody likes that, well some people do but what's wrong with them?" We both laughed as she took my second heel off.

She pushed me back on the bed and told me that she liked my get up and that I looked like an hour glass. I looked at her and whispered, "But you really just want me to be naked right?" She grinned and I knew the answer. So, the get up was soon on my floor. The real fun began or at least I thought it was going to. She had brought something to use as a blind fold but first asked me where my bondage tape was.

I had purchased bright pink bondage tape at the Folsom Street Faire years earlier. She asked if I was saving it for a special occasion and I answered, "Yes, in about two minutes," with a wink. She went to my chest of drawers and found other items including a harness. She looked over at me with an eyebrow raised, "You're going to wear this? Hah! What like some kind of bend over boyfriend thing?" I laughed but truthfully, yes. I had a guy ask me to do that to him once and I did.

Then she's back on the bed and ripping the pink tape. It didn't have much stickiness and I wondered if the adhesive had lessened since I bought it so long ago. Who would think that stuff would expire? It was comical. She ripped a piece off with her teeth and tried to place it on my wrists but it kept folding in on itself. It was a bit of a tangled mess, but I was into it. I was excited about this whole thing after (to come clean) reading Fifty Shades of Grey. You can judge me, I was totally up front about my reading pleasures no matter how badly written they were.

She positioned my (finally) bound hands above my head and retrieved the blindfold. She placed the handkerchief on my eyes first. Then wrapped the belt/blindfold around my head, covering my ears. I said "It's on my ears and I can't hear you." The fact that I couldn't see or hear and my hands were tied, became overwhelming instantly. She could tell I was freaking out and grabbed the blindfold off. Tears gushed from my eyes. I didn't know where that reaction was coming from but it was severe. I was embarrassed but couldn't stop shaking and sobbing. Glyn was calm and rested beside me. She held me and stroked my arm. She told me we didn't have to do any-thing more than just lay with one another. She enjoyed my company no matter what. She said at least the handkerchief could be put to good use and wiped the salty drops off my cheeks.

I appreciated her tenderness and after I collected myself was ready to try again, minus the blindfold. I instead put my arm over my eyes and that worked just fine. I guess it's because I was in control of my arms, who knows, I tried not to think about my outburst and be in the moment.

The sharp strike of the crop against my thigh again, then

softer up and down my ass, inner thigh and then a few gentle nudges on my clit, unexpected but welcome. I then felt the hot wax on my stomach, it traveled to my right thigh then my left. I cringed at the thought of her pouring hot wax on my vagina but I trusted her. She did not pour wax there but higher. She tapped each nipple with the crop as the wax drips slowly on my breasts. I felt a cooling sensation on my nipple as she ate chocolate pudding off the right one. More wax and then cooling on the left. She opened my mouth and fed me a bite of the soft dessert. My eyes still closed I was so turned on and just wanted her to fuck me already. She knew and put her gear on. I was so ready for her. Thinking about all the spankings, wax, licks, it drove me crazy. I begged her to touch me and when I was about to climax, I asked if she'd give me permission to. She did, and my orgasm took me to another atmosphere. I realized that calling her daddy and the whole dom/sub combo added to my desire for her. I had never experienced that before. The daddy name calling wasn't really my thing but it turned her on so I did it.

Later I mentioned something about my sex drive and she said that the people fifteen blocks in one directions and five blocks in the other could feel my sex drive. I was a little embarrassed and then thought, so what, this lady appreciated sex.

We continued a few more weeks but there was a combination of reasons why we stopped seeing each other. I know she wanted more than I could give her and I was never going to feel the way she did.

Glyn helped me realize that I needed and deserved to be adored. I cherished romantic notions and someone wanting all of me. I also realized that it couldn't just be about them wanting me or vice versa. I felt like she was the first one in a long time that wanted me more than I wanted her. I was being pursued instead of doing the pursuing. That part felt good. I had chased people because I had to have the attention. Now, I needed the sincerity behind the chase. I was not interested in game playing, only honesty. I sought fun and sensuality with integrity.

20

The Big 4-0! Turkey, Greece and Italy!

Through my Camino adventure I discovered my wanderlust. I had been intrigued by Greek mythology since I was a child. I read several books and learned about the Gods and Goddesses, even took a course on it in college. I had named myself after the Amazons. The Labrys is a double bladed axe the warrior women used. It is also a lesbian symbol. I loved all the meaning and herstory, I just decided to spell it a little differently. So, needless to say, Greece was calling me. I was determined to turn 40 there. I had quit my job of almost 13 years and was taking myself on a trip of a lifetime, alone in Greece and Italy.

I had always been stubborn against Roman mythology, in my opinion copy caters after the original Greeks. So, I most certainly had to go to Greece before visiting Italy. I found a fantastic flight which had a layover in Turkey. It felt meant to be. I added a few days in Istanbul to my trip. I didn't realize at the time that I was going to countries with so many ancient ruins to celebrate the anniversary of my birth.

I felt so strongly about turning 40 in Greece. After hours

of working on my travel plans I gave in to the idea that I'd be in Italy. I then gave myself a reality check to comprehend how fortunate I was that I was going to be turning 40 in Italy!! I set up my first few places to stay and flights. Once I was in Greece I didn't know how I would get to some of the islands but that's where my sense of adventure soars.

My Wild Turkey Day/Night

With six weeks on my own to explore places I had never been to, my spirit was ecstatic. I packed everything I would need in my trusty backpack and was off.

I arrived in Istanbul in the late afternoon. My Airbnb host had given me clear directions on how to get to her flat. She met me and after a quick tour of the place she showed me around the neighborhood. We had delicious stuffed pitas for dinner as she told me about what I needed to see while visiting. She was going on vacation to Denmark otherwise she would have shown me around herself. I thought that was so kind of her; she had never met me before and was not only willing, but genuinely wanted to make sure I enjoyed her home and city.

The next morning I woke to the sound of the Muslim call to prayer. I knew I was somewhere very different from home. I was a bit jetlagged but more than that there was this openness that overtook me. I was a sponge wanting to soak up my surroundings and loving every second!

I had to see the Hagia Sophia. I was in awe of the exquisiteness and history of the spiritual building. It took me some time to really take in all of its wonder. After my self-guided tour, I wandered around the large square outside. I ate some street food corn on the cob and people watched. Then a young man appeared. He was quite charming and asked if I would like to have tea with him. I said yes and was suddenly in a white room filled with rugs. You know I'm going to say it, so I'm not going to bullshit around, yes, I went to turkey and bought a Turkish rug! I had no intention whatsoever of doing this. I know how touristy that sounds. Even adventurers are tourists sometimes. The part that I was unaware of and I think might only happen to blond American women in their 30's was that my rug came with a young man.

You are probably thinking, what is she talking about? That's what I thought when the man who sold me my 2'x3' woven rug offered me a man in his early twenties. I didn't quite know what to do. It was an unexpected (to say the least!) side journey that I just let life take me on.

I followed the young man up the stairs to a restaurant. Everything was white with fine linens, glasses and plates. I ate fresh vegetables and fish with a glass of sweet white wine. He wasn't hungry and talked about how he was in college. He went on to tell me about his adoration of older American women. He had dated a 30 year old redhead while she was visiting and he liked learning about America. He then started asking me about my life and why I was in Istanbul. He had suggestions of places for me to visit, similar to my host from the Airbnb. I finished my meal and then he asked if I wanted to continue our date. I was going along for the ride and said yes.

We ended up at a pay by the hour motel. As I walked up the stairs I thought to myself, "What the hell are you doing?"

Aren't you done with men? Clearly this trip was looking like a continuation of my last one. After our showers (customary in the Muslim religion, I had learned on Mallorca) and or brief handjobs, we made our way back down the stairs.

Outside he asked if I had any money for a package of cigarettes. I am not a fan of smoking but I obliged. I asked if he would take some selfies with me and he smiled and said in his Turkish accent, "Of course, I would love to." We smiled into my phone with the Hagia Sophia in the background; me with my pink and blond hair and he with his dark eyes and neatly trimmed black beard. We kissed each other on the cheek and said goodbye. It was very surreal and it was only the beginning of my first full day in Istanbul!

In a daze from what had just happened, I decided to see more of the city. I had heard about the baths. A Turkish bath in Turkey, how could I pass up that opportunity?! With my trusty map I made my way to *Cagaloglu Hamami*. I was beckoned in by the marble walls, gold Islamic writing and pictures of famous people that had frequented the bath.

Inside, everything was gold. I thought I had travelled back in time. I was surrounded by more marble, music I didn't understand and a calmness I had never witnessed. I had to wait as I didn't have an appointment but that meant I could sit and have tea. The menu even had gold lettering. Luckily, they had one in English, I chose rose hips tea. I received my own glass teapot with a gold handle (of course) and silver and gold flowers. I sipped my sweet hot tea out of my glass mug and took in the atmosphere.

When it was my turn I entered the women's only area and

undressed in my own room. I made my way toward the show-ers and into the main bath area. Talk about being transported to another time! I thought I had entered into another universe where I was some kind of Goddess. There were eight stone slabs surrounding one in the middle. On the stone in the cen-ter was a woman. I was mesmerized by her. I couldn't help but stare at her long waves of chestnut hair, sun browned skin and the curves of her stretched out body. I was surrounded by other goddesses and women bathing them. A woman came up to me and said hello, her English limited but I was apprecia-tive for any. She asked me to lay down on a marble slab.

Let me just say that there is nothing on this planet like a Turkish woman scrubbing the heck out of your body. I was a rag doll and princess all in one. After all the slathering of soap she rinsed me off with a hose and then rubbed lotion all over me. My skin had never felt as polished, smooth and soft as it did in that moment.

High off that experience the only thing I knew was that I needed to eat. Elated after my dinner and my day I went in search for a taxi. I was near the *Sultan Ahmet Camii* (Blue Mosque) and a man asked if I was looking for a taxi. I said yes and life continued to take me on the journey of that day.

I ended up walking with him toward the mosque where he took pictures of me and us together. He asked if I'd like to see his restaurant. Yes was the answer of the day, so we proceeded. After saying hello to everyone, we climbed up the stairs to the rooftop. It had the best view of the whole city. As I looked at all the lights he took my hands and kissed me. I felt like I was in a dream. I don't know how long it lasted. I think time stands still when you are living in a fantasy sequence.

Somehow we ended up sitting at a front row table at a festival with a Whirling Dervish. I got dizzy just watching him. I could not grasp how the man could make his body spin that fast. Next we went to a bar and we drank raki (it's like ozo with a light licorice flavor). After drinking a few glasses and talking to the bartender that knew him, he said we should go. Outside he suggested we go dancing or to a hotel and have sex all night. Well, we both knew where that story was headed.

The half Italian, half Turkish 32 year old wore this almost 40 year old out! We had sex six times that night. I have never done it that many times. Plus, we had to bath after each time. I showered and casual sexed myself out! He was quite an intense lover. Everything was very hard and forceful. It was sexy but also intimidating. By the morning I was exhausted and honestly wanted to get away from him. He kept calling me his queen. I know it sounds sweet but it freaked me out. He wanted to be my tour guide but I trusted my gut and wanted to continue my adventuring solo. I told him I needed to go back to my place to shower and change. When he contacted me a few hours later I thanked him for the night but that I needed to be on my own.

The rest of my time in Istanbul I did so much exploring! I immersed myself in all the yummies at the Grand Bazaar; from the vibrant spices to Turkish delight candy to glass tea sets with tulips. I made my way across the Bosporus and wandered around the Istanbul Modern museum.

On my last day I went to the *Sultan Ahmet Camii.* It's a

functioning mosque and women need to have their heads covered. That was a memory I will not soon forget. I stood in line for over an hour to be able to enter the place of worship. I respect other cultures and also can't condone the way women are treated in some. I of course would cover my head out of respect but I made sure a couple of pink curls were visible right underneath my silver head scarf. Even though I see myself as spiritual and not religious, I appreciated all the hours it took human hands to make such a stunning space. It's also known as the Blue Mosque for all the blue mosaic tiles inside. All of the detail that went in to making the columns, rounded ceilings and archways was magnificent.

Later that day I boarded my flight to Athens, my dream destination. I couldn't believe all that I had already experienced. I was only in the first few days of my six week exploration and I was on my way to the place I had thought about for decades!

My long anticipated Destination: GREECE

I literally pinched myself when I saw the sign at the airport that read: Welcome to Athens. I couldn't believe I was actually there. I made my way to meet Juno who I would be living with for the next five days. Upon arriving at her apartment she wasn't there. I was disappointed at first. But then loved that I got to look at all of the cool stuff at my own pace.

The kitchen cabinets were painted bright salmon with lime green trim. The bathroom had white tiles with pink flowers and green stems to match the lime green sink. My bedspread was golden and there was a Gustav Klimt print above it. This was so my type of place! When I saw her poster with the female symbol and something to do with feminism I knew she and I would get along.

Juno arrived later that evening and my instincts were correct. She was so warm, we became instant friends. She helped me plan the rest of my trip to the Greek islands of Santorini and Crete. She was born on Crete and told me to spend more time in Chania instead of the capitol of Heraklion. I was so grateful to heed her advice.

While in Athens I visited the Acropolis. It was of course spectacular. But my side trip to Delphi was the most memorable. I had no idea how I would get there but something was pulling me to the oracle at Delphi. After a three hour bus ride I made it. When I walked up to the, "navel of the world," I smiled, it was an outie!

I continued on to explore Apollo's temple and another amphitheater even larger than the one at the Acropolis. Then I came to the Oracle. No, there was no goddess telling me about a vision or my future, unfortunately. What was there though, was an indescribable energy. I believed in all the myths and legends that I had read so many times. I knew at some point, in some reality people came here for answers and received them.

What I didn't know until I got there was that across the road was the temple of Athena. Once arriving at the temple I was stunned. I couldn't move for a minute. Once I regained some composure, I walked around the ruins. I had been there before. You might not believe in past lives and I can understand that. I have had a hard time believing in them myself but a past life is the only way to describe what I felt there. I was attached to it like nowhere else I had visited. I wanted to touch all of the cold broken stone.

When my flesh encountered the stone, chills when up my arm. I closed my eyes and saw darkness with only torches lit held by women in robes chanting. It was a ritual paying tribute to the Goddess Athena and I was part of it. I quickly opened my eyes. I was back in the daylight with a few strangers mulling around the two-toned columns where the plaster had worn away and the stone was exposed. The only thing I could do was sit on a stone and rejoice internally that I was there. As it started to get dark I knew I had to get the last bus back to Athens. I said goodbye once again to one of the most ancient spiritual places. I knew what a tremendous honor it was to be there.

From Athens I took a large ferry to the island of Santorini. I chose that island because I had been captivated by a picture of the sapphire blue domes on top of the crisp white homes. When I arrived I was not disappointed. They were even more stunning in person. I watched a pink and purple sunset at a restaurant overlooking the Mediterranean. All I could see was azure water and islands surrounding me that were created by the volcano. I was in the largest caldera in the entire world. I sat there eating my tzaiki (cucumber yogurt dip) with pita bread and sipped on Greek wine. I felt like the luckiest lady in the world.

The next day I was part of an excursion that took a smaller boat around the island. I hiked up a volcano before boldly jumping into the chilly Aegean Sea. I then swam to a natural hot springs that had the faint smell of Sulphur. I felt extremely proud of myself that day. It might not sounds super adventurous but I was afraid of putting my face in the water and not swimming fast enough to reach the hot springs in time. I almost drowned as a child and having my face under water isn't something I do often. So, being in a foreign city with strangers and in an unfamiliar sea, was a huge accomplishment. The hike was no easy task for me either, up and down an allegedly dormant volcano in a certain amount of time to make sure the boat didn't leave. They were small triumphs and they were all mine.

The last place I went to in Greece was the island of Crete. The history of the Amazons is what drew me there. I wanted to see the ancient ruined Palace of Knossos and had no idea I would stumble upon the ruin of the hall of the double bladed axes! That was something I had never even dreamed of. To me the labrys was a symbol of women's collective empowerment from the warrior women. To happen upon an ancient hall that I had named myself after, was fate whispering to me like it does now and again. I was exactly where I supposed to be. I was living the life I was supposed to be living.

After leaving, Heraklion, I took the most beautiful bus ride I've ever taken through the northern part of Crete, going west to Chania. With the gorgeous green hills and beautiful blue sea, I came upon another epiphany. My heart had healed enough to be able to be broken again. I in no uncertain circumstances wanted it broken, but I could handle it. I had gone through a myriad men. I needed them to feel beautiful, wanted, someone worth attention. Every single one helped me with that. I had no regrets whatsoever! On the bus ride I discovered I wanted more then what I'd been searching for in the past few years. I wanted to be adored and deserved to be. My desire? To have my special someone's whole self, beam when I walked in the room.

When I reached Chania, I got lost finding the studio apartment I was to have all to myself. All the street signs were in two forms of Greek, neither that I could read. Luckily, I kept going back to my directions and was in contact with the woman's brother that I was renting from. After over an hour of walking with my heavy pack I heard a man's voice call out my name. I looked up and saw a welcoming smile. I didn't even notice that my studio was less than one hundred feet from the sea! Inside, they had written on a little chalk board, "Welcome Labris!" and had a small bottle of Raki with a glass as a welcome gift for me. The studio was filled with light. The kitchen was a buttercup yellow and the ceiling had exposed wooden beams. I even had a tiny balcony.

The following day I went on a tour where I got to touch the olive tree where the original olive branch for the Olympic Games came from. The tree was estimated to be over 3000 years old and the oldest living olive tree in the world. She was magical. It felt like I was in the presence of Mother Nature when I placed my palm on her giant thick trunk.

The tour continued to a winery and an olive oil plant. The highlight, besides the ancient tree, was a homemade Greek lunch. We all sat along a large rectangular table outside a couple's house. It was very traditional where the wife cooked everything and her husband of forty some years entertained us with stories. It was some of the best Greek food I had ever eaten. The salad was fresh with big chunks of tomato and feta cheese. It was drizzled with an olive oil dressing and all the flavors burst deliciously in my mouth. The main course was a marinated chicken with peas, squash and potatoes in their homemade tomato sauce. The dessert was like nothing I had ever tasted. It was a cheesecake with a citrus gelatin on top. Suspended in the yellow gelatin were with carrots shaped like crinkle cut French fries.

I ended my day by climbing into my comfortable bed around 10pm. I watched a few minutes of Greek "wheel of fortune," and then Greek "how to become a millionaire." I was so entertained and I don't think it was just the Raki.

I had dinner two night in a row up the cobble stoned street from where I was staying. It was a tiny bistro carved out of stone. The food was fantastic and they brought me a bottle of wine and dessert that came with each dinner special. I liked that they didn't care I was eating alone, I still got the bottle and I drank it while sending pictures of my food and recapping my day to friends.

I loved the way things fell into place on my solo voyage I hadn't known that Chania was a Venetian village and from there I was going to actual Venice, Italy. It was the first time I had heard about this inexpensive airlines that traveled to and from European cities. My flight from Greece to Italy was less than $60!

Italia!

When I first laid eyes on Venice I knew I was somewhere like nowhere else. The streets were made of water! I know they are canals but it's such a cool concept I couldn't get over it.

I booked a walking tour where I learned so much about the city. Tours were the way for me to be around other people and learn about my new environment. I loved taking in all the knowledge the tour guides offered.

A gondola ride was part of the tour which was fortunate for me because they had a two passenger rule. I felt, how ridiculous, you should be able to a ride a gondola by yourself. Anyway, riding on a gondola in Venice was a dream I never thought would manifest in my realty. Beholding Venice by looking up from the canals was astounding. Whose life was I living? Ah! It was my own!

Later that night I attended a silly but informative performance that taught me the vast and colorful history of *Venezia*. All of these reasons and more is how I fell in love with, "the floating city."

I was sad to leave Venice, but also ecstatic to explore another part of Italy. I had already booked a place to stay in *Vernazza* (part of *Cinque Terre*) on the northern west coast. I had seen gorgeous pictures with brightly colored homes and heard you could walk to all five cities (*cinque terre*). Again, I was not disappointed in my choice of destination based on pictures. The first night I was there, I went on an exploration to a wine bar that overlooked the sea. I climbed up about a two hundred tiny steps (I'm not exaggerating) to reach it. It was worth every, single, step. The view of the pristine glass like water was spectacular. The owner was also the waiter and brought me many wines to choose from along with mouthwatering olives and bread. Overlooking the sea with the taste of delicious red wine, while the sunset, was something I didn't want to end.

A couple of hours later the sun already disappearing, I made my way back down the numerous steps and back to my apartment.

I explored two other of the five cities the following day. I was a bit disappointed that after an earthquake you could not walk to all five cities anymore. I was able to take a boat to the ones I was unable to walk to which turned out even better because I could view the cities from the gorgeous, calm water.

That night I sat down to dine alone, as per my usual. An American couple sat down at the table next to me and the husband asked if I was alone. I answered that I was and he asked if I'd mind if they joined me. What a pleasant surprise! We dined on juicy ripe tomatoes with basil and fresh mozzarella to start. Many courses followed including: shrimp skewers covered in Greek herbs, squid ink pasta with fish, fresh fettucine with vegetables and marinara sauce. We then had two desserts. One was a chocolate cake with chocolate fudge and powdered sugar. The other, the restaurants gelato with made to order berry sauce that they pour over the gelato at your table. I was in culinary heaven and so appreciative because without my dinner companions I wouldn't have been able to try so many things.

It was also the first time I had *limoncello*. We had wine throughout dinner but they insisted we have a *digestivo*. I was happy to indulge in this Italian tradition. It took me another few nights to gain the courage to try grappa. I found it to be liquid satin running down my throat as long as I sipped it. Sipping was key!

From Vernazza I took a train to Florence. I would be turning forty years old in *Firenze*! I could never have imagined it. If someone would have told me that I would be in a cooking class making pizza & gelato without a partner but with a cute chef & couples from Memphis & Singapore on my birthday, I would have said they were mad! But, that is just what I did after taking myself to a spa for a manicure & pedicure.

The kitchen we met at was in what looked like a stone castle. The grounds were sprawling and I wished I could have seen it in better light. Once in the kitchen, we were given aprons and shown how to roll the dough, add our ingredients, etc. I also learned that the twenty something instructor had not only heard of Santa Cruz but had visited the summer before. We talked about the movies the boardwalk plays from June-September. What a small world. While our pizzas and calzones were baking, he taught us the difference between gelato and ice cream. Obviously he felt gelato was the superior choice. We then adding all the ingredients for our vanilla bean gelato. What a high caloric, delicious feast. Happy 40th birthday to me!

The real reason I was in Florence was for the famous art. I was able to see "The Birth of Venus," one of my favorite paintings. My gypsy-souled mother was a huge fan of art. Botticelli was one of her favorite artists and a postcard of the, "Birth of Venus," was in our bathroom growing up. When I stood in front of her in her giant clam shell, it felt surreal. I ended up finding a postcard of her in the gift shop that I put up in my bathroom when I returned home.

I had no idea that my reaction to seeing Michelangelo's, David, would literally make my jaw drop. He is quite a sight to behold, exquisite doesn't even come close. I must have looked at him for at least a half hour while taking pictures from various angles. I could not believe he was created from one slab of marble. It sounds like an overreaction, but it isn't. There is just something about that sculpture.

Besides the Airbnb, the phenomenal art, and my birthday cooking class, I was a little disappointed in Florence. It was another big city. I think I had my expectations too high with years of hearing about Tuscany and how amazing Florence was. I had tried going out to eat and was rejected several times because I was alone. Traveling solo was something I enjoyed at least 90% of the time. Eating alone was still hard for me and the repeated rejection made that 10% feel very present.

I was staying at an Airbnb with a couple that had an adorable Pitbull lab mix. He was a great condolence and I don't think it was only for the pizza I brought back from up the street. That tiny pizza shop (more like a garage) was a life saver. There was something about the sauce. I decided to take it as a sign to save money and appreciate being in my Airbnb instead of out at some restaurant. I also got to have leftover pizza for breakfast the next morning. When I woke up, my sadness was gone and I was pleased that I had chosen to add a couple of days in Siena.

Gnocchi Wasn't the Only Thing Served on That Italian Table

I entered the Café Duomo exactly at noon because that's when it opened. I had made the mistake of not eating and even more detrimental, not having caffeine that morning. I had chosen this place because it was right around the corner from the sightseeing I wanted to do at the Siena Cathedral. As I walked through the glass door I saw him immediately. He was bent over writing something, his black pants hugged tight against his firm, small ass. His white, ironed long sleeved shirt loose around his lean, muscular arms. My eyes then led to his head of thick, dark, short hair. He looked up at me, dark coffee eyes sparkled as his wide smile took me by surprise. I asked for a table for one and he replied I could sit wherever I wished.

There was a gentleness about the way he moved from table to table and a friendliness in his voice. After sitting and reviewing the menu he came over and looked directly into my eyes and asked what I would like. I wanted to say, "You!" but instead ordered a cappuccino. I knew I liked those and honestly didn't know the difference between a cappuccino and a latte at that point. Cappuccino sounded more Italian to me. I ordered the gnocchi and throwing caution to the wind some house white wine.

From my previous travels I found that you can order a glass of wine but if you are a wine drinker it's a better deal to order at least a ¼ liter, which is what I did. A guilty feeling crept into the pit of my stomach at the thought of being tipsy when going into the cathedral. The feeling dissipated when Leo, short for Leonardo, started talking to me with his sexy Italian accent. There was only one other person in the restaurant so he felt free to speak to me from across the room. He asked where I was from and we made small talk.

He brought out the cappuccino that he had made setting it down right in front of me so I noticed the large heart in the foam. There were also two packets of sugar on the saucer with the writing, "Keep calm and don't worry," and "Keep calm and feel good." I began to wonder if he was flirting with me. I wasn't looking for another love affair, but this one found me.

He next brought out the gnocchi which was covered in a greasy tomato sauce with several pieces of bacon on top. This was not what I expected but he was so gorgeous I didn't want to seem rude or unappreciative. I instead took a giant sip of the white wine he had set on my red placemat. He was cleaning a table to my right and casually mentioned that young people hung out in the piazza where there were bars and good music after dark. I smiled politely and nodded. He then continued that we should go there tonight and get a drink once he was done with work.

A piece of gnocchi almost flew out through my nose, I was so shocked. I was glad he wasn't looking directly at me in that moment. Someone had entered the restaurant and he greeted them with a warm smile and showed them to a table. Did I imagine the previous conversation? Maybe he was just being nice and didn't mean it in a flirty way? Taking pity on a lonely traveler perhaps? I continued to eat the overly salty gnocchi in silent excitement and grinned between sips of caffeine and alcohol. When I finished my wine he brought over another ¼ liter this time of champagne and said it was from him with a wink. Oh my god he did ask me out, what was I going to do?

After I paid and was gathering myself to leave I thought, "Should I bring up tonight, am I going to actually meet him, is this safe?" and so many other questions. I needn't have bothered with any of the internal anxiety because he nonchalantly mentioned that he wasn't off work until around midnight and could I meet him back at the restaurant then. Relieved and exhilarated I smiled and nodded in agreement. He then did the customary Italian kiss on each cheek and I swear there was electricity in the stubble of his 5 o'clock shadow. I breathed in the rich scent of his masculinity and expensive cologne and didn't know how I would be able to resist.

I wandered around the sweet city and then went back to my shared Airbnb. I had gotten along great with the woman who lived there and rented out her extra room. Even though I was excited and filled with anticipation, I thought maybe I was being too spontaneous. Maybe meeting him at midnight wasn't safe.

She was in the kitchen making coffee and asked how my day had been. I told her about Leo and asked for her advice. It was priceless, "You are young and only here a few days. Go for it! Otherwise won't you just be here, bored?" She said she knew people in town and that I had her phone number if I needed it. Her enthusiasm sealed the deal. Her and her boyfriend even showed me how to call a taxi before I left later that night.

The rest of the day was a blur of me figuring out what to wear, makeup, etc. Then we smiled at each other through the windows of the cafe at midnight. He was almost done and offered me in to have a glass of *vino rosso*. His coworker waited for her ride and smiled at me sweetly. I wondered if she was secretly judging me as a blond American harlot or laughing at me because he did this all the time, or both. I didn't care because I was going to spend the evening with a tall, dark and handsome Italian man at least ten years my junior!

As soon as she left he sat down next to me and poured himself a glass of wine. We got through a few sips, some chit chat about our days, as much as we could not knowing each other's language very well. Then, he leaned over and gently but firmly kissed me. His lips were full and soft, his mouth warm, wet and hungry. I didn't want it to end and when it did he confessed that he had wanted to kiss me earlier but he was shy with people around. Wow! Yes, I would have been embarrassed with a bunch of strangers staring at me while my waiter kissed me like that. He smiled flirtatiously, called me "Bella", then grabbed the wine and our glasses and said we should go to the upper part of the restaurant so no one could see us. I didn't even know there was an upper area.

In the upstairs dining area he set everything down, pulled me close to him and began kissing me. We were standing and I was pressed up against a two person sized table. All of a sudden my dress was off and his shirt and pants gone. We were both in our under garments with hands groping from dark hairy chest to size DD bra. He leaned down to take off his dark blue boxer briefs and uncovered the largest penis I had ever seen. I swear that thing went down to his knee. For a moment I thought, where does he think that thing is going to go? He was so hot and our chemistry could have caught that entire restaurant ablaze, so that worry left as soon as it entered my mind. I took off my carefully chosen red satin bra and matching thong panties. As I did, he cleared one of the tables and proceeded to pick my naked ass up and set me on it. There was grabbing, squeezing, and hair pulling as his head slowly disappeared between my thighs. His tongue was definitely not a novice in that area.

After a few minutes his face reappeared and he went to get a condom. I couldn't believe I was having sex on a table in a restaurant in Siena, Italy! I was sitting and he was standing, then we moved to a chair and I was on top. His strong Italian hands caressing my back and ass as we moved up and down with one another. He climaxed and I thought that wooden chair was going to collapse under the strain of our passion.

When we were done he asked if I wanted to spend the night with him at his flat. Had I been granted a secret wish that I didn't know about? "Are you kidding me? Hell, Yes!" was my inside answer. But I simply replied, "I would like that very much, thank you." As I got dressed, he proceeded to put the table setting back on the table we had just had sex all over. Thank god for place mats!

Upon arriving at his one bedroom flat, he was quite the gentlemen and offered me another drink and something to eat. All I was ravenous for was more of him. I pinched myself when he wasn't looking. I couldn't believe I was in a twenty-something year old beautiful Italian man's apartment. After the short tour of his place we went directly to his room. We were naked again and the kissing was no longer soft and tender but powerful and full of wantonness. He pleasured me with his fingers and when my moans of ecstasy were over I climbed on top of him.

We rolled over and over and every which way on his queen sized bed. He spoke to me in Italian which was heaven to my ears. I had no idea what he was saying and that made it even hotter. He looked at me intensely as he reached his peak, his obsidian eyes then closing to fully enjoy his release. We laid in each other's arms for many sweet and sensual minutes before he asked what side of the bed I wanted to sleep on.

We watched Italian bloopers on his bedroom television while touching arms and feet, slowly getting sleepy. I started to fall asleep first and he turned off the television and the light. I felt totally safe with him. I was correct with my first impression. He was a gentle soul albeit with a sexy beast alter ego. I slept without interruption until his alarm sounded the following morning or should I say a couple of hours later.

He had to be at the restaurant at ten o'clock to get ready for the twelve o'clock lunch crowd. What a difference one day makes, I thought to myself as I quickly showered in his bathroom. Looking around I observed his good quality shampoo, body wash and shaving cream, not to mention the variety of colognes. This young man knew how to take care of himself, and he had definitely taken care of me only a few hours prior.

I walked with him to the restaurant and we kissed one another good bye. I said I would come by the following day to say goodbye before catching my bus to Rome but I didn't have time. I knew ours was a one night fling and that was perfecto. I waved to him while he opened the restaurant door and a little smile came a crossed my face remembering that I had chosen the café only 26 hours earlier purely because of its location. I had been a hungry, 40 year old, curvaceous, California woman in search of some Italian food having no idea of how the day would unfold. I smelled him on me for hours as

I walked through the cobblestoned streets of Siena, fully satiated, and I wondered what life would bring next.

Roma

I had the opposite experience from Florence as far as expectations in Rome. I don't know if it was my love of Greece or the hype that Rome had that made me not very excited to visit. I had to fly out there to get home so I broke down and decided to be a tourist and stay a few days. To my complete surprise, Rome is fantastic! The hype is real!

Before I even entered my Roman apartment I noticed that there was a gourmet *gelateria* only a few feet away. This was already the perfect place to stay. I took the key from the lock box and as soon as I entered the apartment I was greeted by a giant wall with "Welcome," in various language and colors. Upstairs in the bedroom loft there was a red wall and a bed with a comforter that was white with red kiss marks. It was so much fun!

I had seen on a map that the apartment was close to the Colosseum. I am directionally challenged and couldn't figure out at first where the Colosseum was. I decided to walk down my street and when I reached the end of the long block I was wondering if I had chosen the right direction. I turned to my left and I could see it. It was massive! And it was only three blocks away. I made my way towards it and even in person it didn't seem real. I couldn't believe the archways and columns had lasted throughout so much of human history. But today's reality came back when I noticed the soldiers carrying machine guns. I was definitely not in California.

I took a tour of the Colosseum and the surrounding areas.

We walked around the other ruins built by emperors first, before ending with the Colosseum. The massive ruins, gardens and statues were tremendous.

We then made our way to what I had so looked forward to. We walked up many flights of stairs in the massive structure and learned about its brutal and deadly history. I knew most of what the tour guide told us, but being there made it too real. It was quite an architectural achievement but I felt uneasy. The centuries of destruction and death haunted me. I could feel the agony oozing out of the walls. I needed to get out of there as quickly as possible.

Running down the stairs as soon as the tour finished, I headed back to my place. I felt like I needed to take a shower and wash all of it off me. I then made my way to the gelateria to cleanse myself with sugar and Italian cream!

The following day I visited the Vatican. I had to see the art, most importantly the Sistine Chapel. I took a tour and was able to see "La Pieta" and the numerous gold and jeweled covered statues. The tour guide informed us that the Pope would be speaking the next morning and anyone could come. That peaked my interest. My grandmother tried to raise me Catholic but that didn't fly with my parents. Even though I wasn't religious I still thought the idea of getting to see him would be a chance of a lifetime. I kept it in the back of my mind and continued looking at the floors filled with art.

I decided to see the Sistine Chapel on my own. They only let so many people in at a time and luckily I wasn't there at a super busy time. Stepping into the chapel I was immediately covered in the presence of the miraculous. The paintings on the ceiling were phenomenal. I stood there, my mouth gapping. How was this humanly possible? Again, I am a spiritual person, not religious, but I felt the divine helped Michelangelo out with that one. I don't even know how long I stood, trying not to blink at this supernatural creation.

I hadn't heard about the paintings of the two sides of the chapel. One side was the life of Moses and the other was the story of Jesus. Beautiful images everywhere. There were a lot of people and I couldn't believe that they just looked around for a minute or two and then left. I could have stayed in there all day.

At one point I was going to sit in a chair and I don't know what happened but in the middle of the Sistine Chapel I fell to my knees. It was quiet and then I made a ruckus when I fell. I thought about quickly scrambling to the chair with peoples help but I stayed there on my knees for a few extra seconds. The religious symbolism was not wasted on me. Once in the chair, I was a little embarrassed but mostly tried to figure out what had just happened. I had fallen on my knees in the Sistine Chapel. That is what happened. Something about that made me start to think about my life. So, I sat in the Sistine Chapel and contemplated life while peering up at images of God.

I did not turn into a religious person. I did spend hours going over the many signs, miraculous moments and magic voyages that I had lived through the past few years. I was trying very hard to live in the moment, but reminiscing and thinking about my future once I left this amazing country, was on my mind. I went to sleep contemplating if I should try and see the Pope.

The following day I woke up early with the hope that, yes, I might be able to be in the presence of the Pope. When I arrived at the Vatican there were plenty people there but it wasn't a mad house by any means. They had to areas with metal detectors that you walk through and that was it. I thought if this was the United States the security would be at least twenty times this.

I was able to walk right through and stood wondering what would happen. About a half an hour later with much more people I noticed officials from the Vatican stepped onto the designated speaking area. Then everyone started shouting, "Papa!" with excitement and getting their phones and cameras out. About two minutes later the Pope was riding in his Pope mobile only two people lines in front of me! I could have almost touched him! It was like seeing a superstar or something.

The energy there was so full of hope and joy. Once he rode through the crowd a couple of times, he went up to his area and sat down. There were a few other speakers before he stood at the podium. His sermon was in Italian. I don't know what he said and might not have agreed with all of it. I don't agree with the Catholic Church on many things. But, if I was going to be in the presence of a Pope that was the one I'd choose. At the end of his talk he blessed us all including all of our loved ones. A blessing from the Pope felt like an awesome way to end my six week adventure.

My last night in Rome was not my last night in Rome

When I arrived at the airport in Rome, there was a smell in the air and I wondered why it was so foggy. I didn't notice until my taxi sped away that there were people roaming around aimlessly. I stood there, half asleep at 5am wearing my 25 pound backpack, newly purchased lime green leather purse and completely touristy shoulder bag that had Italia in several colors all over it. I stood there wondering what was going on.

I followed the crowd to the terminal I thought I would be flying out of in just a few hours. I was told by another American that she was told there was a fire. Seriously, a fire in Rome. The idea of Rome burning was just too classic for me not to appreciate. Where was Nero and his fiddle? I was humored by it until I learned the fire started in a restaurant in my terminal, which spread to another and therefore, no flights would be leaving that day.

I took a deep breath, and exhaled into bewilderment. The only person I knew was my Airbnb host and his place was booked for the rest of the week. The fog that surrounded me was actually billowing smoke and now people were starting to freak out and hunt for cabs. I had no idea where to start figuring out my situation. I followed other people. As we walked, the sun started to rise. Walking, always walking, this was one of the few times I really wished I was with someone I knew, someone that loved me and would handle this and take care of me. Ugh, why was I here alone? Boo! I totally booed the entire situation, including feeling sorry for myself. Yuck, I despise that feeling. Another deep breath. Girl you better figure this shit out fast, nobody's coming to save your ass. Stop moping and get to rescuing yourself. It's Rome for goodness sake, not the depths of the Amazon or the middle of the desert.

Still a little pouty, I looked around, and even with all the people wandering about I noticed what looked like an available cab. There was someone to help me; an older Roman man that spoke no English except where would I like to go. I asked to go to a hotel by the Colosseum. I had heard of the Radisson. He smiled and shook his head yes. As we drove I just wanted a bed and to know when I was going home. When we reached the Colosseum he stopped the cab and smiled again. When I looked back at him he asked where to and I said I didn't know. I realized it was the beginning of high tourist season and many people would be unexpectedly stranded in Rome. I got nervous.

He took me to a hotel and they were booked. He drove me to another, they were booked. The third one was a 4 star hotel with availability. When he found out they had vacancies he left before they told me it was 290 euro a night! The concierge saw the look on my face and offered to call two other places that were within walking distance. He found me something around the corner and when I walked in the man was as nice as he told me the premium room that was ready for 280 euro. He would give me a discount to make it 250. At that point I was so exhausted and in need of the internet to figure out my life, I agreed to it. I had never paid that much to stay in a hotel. As I crawled into that bed at 6:30 in the morning not having been able to get any news about my flight, it was clearly worth every euro.

After sleeping for a few hours I went down to the Internet

station because my phone wasn't working. I checked my email and there was nothing new from anyone. I decided to check an old email and read that my flight was delayed 5 hours and 50 minutes and would be leaving in 10 minutes! My heart raced, stomach churned, obscenities screamed in my mind.

After what seemed like an hour I regained composure and called the airlines. To make a long story even longer, after three hours and a metro trip to the Turkish airline office which was luckily only five metro stops away, I managed to procure myself a seat on a flight at the exact same time the following day. The pleasant airline receptionist even told me that not only were there no costs to change flights, they would reimburse my hotel cost. I got to stay an extra day in Rome for free at a fantastic four star hotel! Later that evening, the hotel served fabulous purple cocktails in giant martini glasses by the roof top pool which just happened to overlook the Colosseum.

Roman Cab Driver

In disbelief that I was actually going home that morning when I gingerly placed my unpainted toes on the nice carpet, I did the all-too-familiar morning routine. I usually wasn't so tired but it was the second day in a row getting up in Rome around 4:15am. I had packed the little that I had unpacked of my backpack the night before. I had showered and laid out my clothes along with my trusty hiking boots. They looked so new after all the places, climates and terrains I had worn them through.

The cab driver was already waiting for me when I arrived downstairs. He took my backpack and set it in the trunk as he told me his name was Frederico. Once in the car he continued to chat. He owned the cab business and was quite proud of himself. He wanted to make one million dollars by the end of the year and was already well on his way. Most people would have been impressed by this, but I wasn't. I was half asleep and thought, "He's cute, but why does he have to talk?"

I was nervous and excited to be finally going home after the ordeal yesterday. I had hoped I might be able to sleep some of the 40 minute drive. When he told me his real passion was the tango, I knew I would be awake the entire way. He also wanted me to know that he wasn't just Roman, his father was Argentinian. He had black rimmed glasses, wavy dark hair, and was about 25. He mentioned again that his name was Frederico and besides the tango he was also learning Thai massage.

I somehow managed to get a word in that I was from near San Francisco and going home today. He remarked that he liked San Francisco and had lived there for two years. I made the mistake of asking how he ended up there. His reply was not at all expected. "I met these women. They were lesbians. You have heard of lesbians?" I couldn't help but chuckle and wanted to say, "I've been familiar with their work since 1995." It was 4:45am and I was not that quick. Instead I mumbled, "Yes, I have heard of them." He continued, "So these ladies, these lesbians, had a big house in San Fran and invited me to live with them and be their boyfriend." I laughed, "They weren't very good lesbians, were they?" But he didn't get my humor. He went on, "So, they were very good to me. I was able to go to school and practice my tango as well as being a stripper at the Wild Honey Club. Do you know it? It was a bar during the day and a strip club at night?" I did not know it and he was shocked and disappointed in my character, which I found very humorous.

He told me he was so young back then. Now he was the ripe old age of 27 with a belly and "these glasses." What a baby, 27! How adorable, he thought he was old. He'll learn, I thought to myself. I told him I was 40 and he said he thought I was 32. I have always appreciated the flattery of being told I look younger even if it's just from someone who wanted to get into my pants. After he finished with his story he asked if I had a boyfriend. I told him no and thought I might as well be honest. I revealed that I had been married to a woman. He wasn't surprised and next asked if I liked men, too. I answered that I did. I was also a bad lesbian. I laughed. Again he didn't find me funny. I shouldn't have encouraged him, but he was hilarious to me after everything I had seen and done over the six weeks. I thought, how perfect that I had flirty cabby as I'm ending my adventures here.

His response to me liking men was priceless, "That is very good." As he shook his head up and down. He went on to say that it was too bad I was leaving because he wanted to give me a free tango lesson. At this point I'm like, sure buddy, I'm sure you'd give me a free "tango lesson." We had reached the airport when he told me that he yearned to practice his Thai massage on me. "Oh, honey", I wanted to tell him, "You wouldn't know what to do with all this woman." But as he was pulling up to the curb I just let him continue.

He turned around and looked at me over his thick black

frames and said he wished we had five more minutes so he could feel my beautiful body with his fingers. "Exactly," I thought to myself, this young thing had no idea what he'd be getting himself into. My response as I opened the door, "Well I need to save something for next time." He made sure he gave me his card before I left the cab and when he handed me my backpack he said, "This is how we say goodbye in Rome", and he kissed me on each cheek. His last words, "I can't wait until next time to show you how Argentinians say goodbye."

21

The Freak-out Before the Calm

After my six weeks away I definitely felt homesickness. Once home, I did go through a bit of a lull. My trip that I had planned for a year was over. I had quit my job of thirteen years and had some leads but nothing full-time. I couldn't plan another trip as I didn't know where my next paycheck was coming from.

I had worked since I was sixteen, scooping ice cream on nights and weekends. Maybe it was because I stepped into my unknown. I jumped off the cliff and was free falling but then realized I could use my wings. Why was I afraid to open them up and let myself fly? I was used to the fear. The idea that lurking out there was desperation, that I wouldn't have a net to catch me.

Taking a giant breath of fresh air into my lungs, releasing it slowly, in and out, in and out, I calmed down. Maybe a few more for good measure. I talked to myself, "You know this is the life you are supposed to be living. The answers are forming, you planned for this. Don't freak out, you are not going to be homeless." A few seconds later my mind started racing.

"Oh my god! I am going to be homeless selling my body on the street giving blow jobs for $20. What the fuck was I thinking quitting my job? Holy shit!!! I have to get a job, I have to get a job, I have to get a job!!!"

So much for consoling myself and remaining calm while I discovered what it was I would be doing with my life now. I told myself that I didn't deserve to go on that trip. How dare I spend money that entire time without earning any? Who the hell did I think I was? I was going to pay for my bravado. There would be no more frivolous spending. I wanted to get my roots colored again. Nope, can't afford it. Oh and going out to eat, I had done quite enough of that in Europe. I definitely didn't deserve that. I was a 40 year old woman changing careers with no direction except she wanted to be a writer and travel the world. Like that's an original idea! Please lady get your head out of your ass and start realizing that you're totally fucked! Or you're going to be in those pretty pink heels if you don't figure this out, like now.

This was what I called hitting my bottom, well not actually hitting it but I was torturing myself into believing I was there. It was not my finest hour or day, but I stayed there for a few. Fortunately, I have close deep friendships and when Dee asked me how I was, "I'm lost," was all I could answer.

I tried to impress her with all the time I had spent on craigslist and researching countless jobs on line for days, not eating well or showering. She looked at me compassion in her eyes, "Oh, you're tormenting yourself." Warm tears cascaded from my eyes as soon as she said it. She knew. I didn't knowhow, but she knew what I had been doing to myself.

"Yes, I guess that's what I've done since I've been home." I spoke through the muffled Kleenex in her embrace. I could not fool her with all of the things I had been shaming myself into doing to "make up" for the fact I got to experience such an adventure.

That night I talked to her about all of it, the fear, the excitement, the unknown of it all. I had lived the same schedule for almost 13 years, through most of my marriage, separation, divorce, and new singlehood. I had gotten up and gone to the same benign, passionless place 40 hours a week, day in and day out. I had remembered that before I left I had taken a leap of faith not in my ability to get another good paying job but in the knowing that my soul knew what I was destined for.

The next day I took a break from the madness of job searching and walked around the garden. The sun yellow roses bloomed in front of my eyes. Their scent gifts flew into my nose as I inhaled and tried to take all of it in. The fluffy white dog below squeaked her multi colored ball. She was being persistent in her efforts to have me chase her because she wouldn't drop the ball. The Siamese kitty from Mexico meowed as she rubbed herself on my left leg. She rolled onto her back in anticipation of a belly rub only to playfully attack when I attempted. Standing up I heard the bees doing their remarkable job on the lavender. I beamed up at the sky so far above this magic scene that I was fortunate enough to call home.

22

Slate

While I figured out how to finance my life as an adventurer, I decided to give romance another shot. I knew I was ready, whether I would actually meet the butch woman of my dreams was another story.

It was a Saturday in early February when I woke up to the sun's rays rippling through my curtains. My first thought, I had had enough of the friends-with-benefits situation and was craving something real or nothing at all. So, after making that declaration I got out of my double bed and took a shower.

As I was foaming up my shampoo I couldn't remember the last time I had bought myself flowers. I was going to cook for myself, too. After getting my sundress, flip flops and hoop earrings on, I left the house in search of worthy, enjoyable things to do for myself.

I picked up a tortilla chicken salad for lunch, I was going to make dinner, there's only so much cooking I can do, I mean really. The yummy café where I bought my salad was around the corner from my favorite flower shack. I had decided that if a bouquet caught my eye I would buy it. As I walked through the flower shack, a metal bucket filled with long stemmed dark peach roses that looked like Nature had dipped them in a lake of fuchsia water, immediately caught my attention. These were the flowers. I was also drawn to stems of flowers with lime green petals. They reminded me that I didn't need anyone to buy me flowers, I was 100% capable and excited to give them to myself.

At home, I arranged the flowers in a purple glass vase on the dining room table and was filled with delight as I gazed upon them while I ate my home cooked dinner.

I then remembered that I had put an app on my phone called "She" the prior June. I had taken it off because it had irritated me for one reason or another. The next idea that popped into my brain was to put the app back on my phone. I had primarily dated men but had fallen in love with and been married to a woman. I knew my connection was with women. I was into butch women. My time with men was done.

I updated my pictures and checked out some of the women in my area. I thought this should just be fun. I wasn't going to take it too seriously after my wonderful morning. Then, like in a movie, I came across this beautiful smile surrounded by redwood trees. She also happened to have blue eyes, which everyone by now already knows are my weakness. I decided to press the pink heart on her picture and then proceeded to go about my day. I presumed the app would notify if I got a "like" or message or something from her or someone else, but nothing all day. Out of curiosity, I decided to check the app in the evening and was nicely surprised that there was a message for me from the butch woman who the smile in the forest belonged to. An electric shock rushed through me and

I couldn't wait to read what she said. She inquired about my name and we messaged back and forth from there until she asked me to coffee a couple of days later.

I pulled up in my mini cooper, only had enough change for 45 minutes on the meter and didn't want to waste time looking for change as I wanted to arrive on time. I was nervous. It felt different than meeting the others. I was drawn to her with this feeling that ran throughout my body, unexplainable except it started in my chest.

I got out of the care in a black long sleeved cotton dress with a baby pink scarf wrapped tightly around my neck. I tried not to run and was elated when I saw that full-toothed smile through the coffee shop window. A smile appeared on my face as well. As I walked toward the door, it opened. She on the other side, invited me in.

Her knee high black lace up motorcycle boots were what caught my eye next. Damn, they were sexy. Her entire presence: 5'10 with short light brown wavy hair, those eyes that shone through her wire-framed glasses and her manners. I'd always had a thing for chivalry. As we sat I noticed the black dragon tattoo crawling up her forearm and the beginning of a grin on her face as she took me in. Something behind those eyes hinted at wanting to devour me. I had to turn away.

The conversation was engaging and thoughtful. I was captivated by her and then realized I had to put money in the meter. I was digging through my purse for another quarter and she handed me her parking card. I found a quarter but was moved by her offer. I had just met her and she was willing to pay not only for my mocha but for my parking. Small, thoughtful gestures really endear me to a person. I don't need diamonds. The knowing that they took their time and thought about me is huge.

We continued our conversation where she informed me that she had two children. In the past I would have had a screaming alarm go off in my head, "Danger danger, beep beeeeeep!!" But the voice instead said, "Okay, she has kids, take a breath, let's just wait and see." I inquired about them. She had a girl who was turning eighteen and a boy who was nine. She had known their father since high school, he was an escape from her tumultuous family life. She knew she was a lesbian since before even dating him but he was her best friend and they ended up married and together for over twenty years. She came out when she turned 40 and realized she couldn't lie anymore.

I told her about my marriage and new life as well. It turned out we had both gone through life transformations the last couple of years. I was nervous to tell her that I had been dating mostly men since my marriage ended because even though I have no shame around it, some lesbians have a hard time and won't date women who they consider bisexual. She was not concerned at all. Her response was who was she to judge? She appreciated men, she just didn't want to have sex with them.

At this point I realized that I had to get to work. She walked me out and as we approached my car, looked at me and said she had a wonderful time and hoped to see me again. She gave me a hug goodbye and I told her I hoped to see her again. We looked at one another as I drove away. I hadn't felt that alive in my heart in years. I was excited and hopeful.

An awesome and intriguing human had just entered my life. At work a half an hour later my phone chimed. She had a great time and wondered if I was available Saturday from 10:00am-1:00pm to meet for hot cocoa and a beach walk. She mentioned that I was beautiful and she especially loved the pink scarf. I might have squealed a little!

We ended up meeting for a drink the next night instead. I spotted her and she was wearing another pair of black leather boots. Turns out blue eyes weren't my only weakness. We sat nursing our cocktails on a purple sofa for three hours, discovering one another. As we talked about the renaissance faire, tattoos and 80's music, our blue jeaned legs began to touch and our hands gently brushed one another's. At one point she took my right hand in her left, not a word uttered, just the action with my fingers squeezing her my approval. At the end of the night she walked me to my car and by my door, under the street lamp, she kissed me. Soft lips, gentle yet strong, I could feel the passion she was keeping under control. We held hands as we kissed. I didn't realize she was bending her legs so she was just the right height. After kissing we held each other in the February night. She looked into my eyes and said I was lovely. We kissed goodbye and I said I hoped we could do more of that the next time we saw each other, to which she agreed. She waited in the parking lot as I drove off. When I got home I received a text thanking me for a delightful evening that I was sweet and delicious.

The next morning, a Saturday, one week since I had bought myself flowers and declared that I didn't need romance in my life. I woke up with the sun in my face again, and decided to text her first. I told her that I was compelled to let her know I thoroughly enjoyed her company last night and I was going to have a huge smile on my face all day. She texted right back that she was seconds away from typing the exact same thing. She admitted that she was completely enamored with me, woke up thinking about me and would probably be thinking about me all day.

Later that day I sent her a picture of the sunset and her response was that I'd been on her mind all day. She had missed her exit because she was thinking of me instead of where she was driving. She then asked me out the Friday before Valentine's Day. I was anxious and eager; we'd only just met, should I get her a gift?

I decided on socks, so sexy I know but I wanted to acknowledge the day but not go crazy. I believed they were thoughtful as they had coffee cups, beans and turquoise hearts on them. I had found out that turquoise was her favorite color and our first date was for coffee. That Friday she picked me up. In her arms were half dozen long stemmed red roses. I almost shrieked out loud! The romantic jester swept me off my feet.

We went to a dreamy spot for dinner with low lights and dark red walls. We fed each other chocolate truffles after our Italian meal as we held hands on the table. We talked later about how we didn't want to rush into bed together, savoring this beginning part was important to us both. That being said we spent the night together a week later.

After the copious amounts of male and female lovers, casual sexual encounters abroad and in my hometown, Slate was the most incredible lover I had ever had. The first time we were together we had sex for over three hours in a cyclone of flesh exploration.

Skin on skin, where I began and she ended I had no idea and it didn't matter. We were in a rhythmic body dance to a song that only the two of us could hear. As we got to know one another, we discovered not only the lingering glances and sweaty after climax spooning, but Slate held my hand as I stepped through the kink looking glass into her arms.

I thought of our relationship as BDSM for beginners. It started out with me buying corsets, a strip tease and lap dance for her. I discovered my body in an entirely new way. I was on all cylinders for hours with her. It wasn't just being tied to her four poster bed with soft black leather handcuffs, blindfolded, wearing metal nipple clamps. I learned that I had a fetish for polishing those big black boots that caught my eye the first time I met her.

Her boots became a ritual. She would bring a cloth bag and towel from her room. She was the dom and I was her sub. She required me to be naked and on my knees, not looking at her as she sat down in an overstuffed brown armchair in her living room. She would hold a riding crop across her lap with a large cat-like grin on her face. I learned that not many femme women subs were bootblackers. Apparently it was a butch thing. I didn't care, there was something about it that turned on every cell in my body.

After I had taken off the laces, dusted both boots, washed them and then polished them, hours had gone by. At the very end, I would re-string her laces, asked if she was pleased and wait for her response. The answer always, "Yes." The cherry on top for us both was the final polishing. I would straddle her boots, one at a time and give them my very own personal shine.

When I was finished she would walk me upstairs and pleasure me however I wanted for as long as I wanted. It was not about restraints at that point but, depending on the day, hard and fast fucking or delicate, soft sex. She helped create a safe place for the kinky piece of me to feel free to come out from the shadows of shame I had pushed my desires to. The yearnings I heard were sick and unacceptable were celebrated with her. I let the years of secret disgrace, and the judgmental voices dissipate with every orgasm she gave me.

A few weeks later, "You've been on my mind all day," followed by a brilliant orange and pink sunset picture on my phone. The next day, only a curt response to one of my text messages. We would only see each other Wednesday and Friday nights, rarely other days and times.

Slate surprised me one Saturday morning at a race I was running, and I was thrilled. I was so moved by the surprise visit because we were always on her time table. I was her everything as long as she wasn't working, exercising or with her children.

One evening over dinner she gave me a green box wrapped with a turquoise bow. I unwrapped it to find a silver chain and pendant in the shape of a leaf with a turquoise stone. She looked into my eyes and asked me to be her girlfriend. I have ever been flippant about commitment. Sharing my time and another person sharing theirs has always felt deserving of depth. When I said "yes," as she placed the necklace around my neck, a piece of my soul blossomed.

A few weeks later I confessed that I was falling for her. She couldn't respond. I had tolerated living on the outskirts of her life until then. We walked around my neighborhood where I told her I needed her to be "all in." She responded that she was and in the same breath, that she wasn't enough for me.

My birthday was two days later. The evening of my birthday Slate took me out to a delicious meal at her favorite restaurant. She bought me a bright pink satin pair of panties with a giant bow. The most thoughtful: she had painted a 24x36 painting of a boganvia flower with shades of burgundy, pink, chartreuse and forest greens. She had even asked my good friend, an artist, to create a drift wood frame for it. I was speechless and falling even more for her. After a night of the best massage I'd ever had and our usual incredible lovemaking, she drove me to the airport. I was going with one of my best friends on a customary birthday trip. We were going to Ireland for eight days.

While I was away I would text her and send her pictures of my trip daily. Besides one phone conversation where she was awkward about my friend being in the room, I didn't hear from her or see her until she picked me up from the airport. We had a tough conversation before I left but I thought we had worked through it.

I was only gone a week and had been in communication so I didn't understand what changed. I was so excited to see her and she was barely there. Three days after my return, on Mother's Day, she asked if she could come over. I knew it was over. She was in tears on my loveseat as she informed me that it just wasn't working for her any longer. She couldn't explain why and I couldn't understand why she couldn't tell me what changed for her. I was in a cloud of confusion. Why couldn't she just be honest with me about why she didn't want to be with me anymore?

The next day she asked if she could come over to talk more. I didn't really want to see her as my heart was hurting. I hoped that at least I would get some clarity. I was wrong. She began to explain that in dom/sub relationships after a "scene" there can be something called "sub drop." It can be an experience that was so intense for the submissive it leaves them feeling needy and depressed. She said that maybe that's why we had that tough conversation weeks prior. In my head I was like, "What the fuck are you talking about?!!" I decided to let her finish her thought, maybe she would get to why she didn't want to be with me anymore. Nope.

After another few minutes of what I felt was nonsense bullshit, I told her that I had not experienced this sub drop and for her to not try and dismiss my feelings. I continued by saying that since we weren't going to be together I'd like to give her the things she gave me back. She was taken aback to say the least. When I handed her the necklace and painting back she was pissed. I explained, "Why would I keep a painting on my wall to remind of how you don't want to be with me? I can't wake up to that." She didn't understand and grabbed it, slammed her minivan door and screeched away.

I stood in front of my house in awe. I thought to myself, "Really, Slate, now you're the victim in this situation, please, spare me." She was a piece of work as far as I was concerned. She was the one that couldn't see me because of her other priorities. She was the one who broke up with me. Now, I was the bad guy because I didn't want her vulva looking painting staring at me day in and day out. Good Riddance!

Of course that was my ever protective anger shielding me from the sorrow I knew would come sooner rather than later. But instead of stifling my tears, I freed them. I came to the consciousness that the sparkling silver lining was that Slate taught me, or rather I taught myself, through the pungent carousel of our relationship, that I was finally capable of falling for someone again. I had let down my guard and let someone in! What that also meant, I could do it again, Hallelujah!

I had "convinced" myself that of course I could fall in love again. But secretly, underneath that rainbow sprinkled layer had been the sticky tar of fear gripping me, telling me that maybe Jay was it. Maybe my years of happiness with her were all I got this lifetime. I so wanted to be covered in the sprinkles but the thick muck was much easier to be stuck in. Was I worthy of anyone else's eyes exuding adoration into mine? Could I feel someone's wanting of me ooze from every pore of their skin?

Slate was the reason I could finally say "yes!" I opened up every part of myself to her, all of her. I think she wanted to love me but for whatever her reasons she couldn't. My only explanation was that she was not my person. The vital role she played was instead, the human that proved I could experience held breaths as I received a text message, heart races as I read her honeyed words and my whole body lit up by her touch. It was a love affair, not a romance or a relationship and it was perfect.

23

Embracing Me

After Slate I was done placing blame on my naïve open heart and trusting soul. Even though I was hurt, the discovery that I could be was what I had been trying to achieve for the last few years. It made me laugh, "Yay! I can be hurt again." But it was that after years of anger, grief and healing, I was able to let myself be vulnerable to real feelings again. Hopefully the next time it would be reciprocated but I was happy to have another chance, whenever that might be.

When I left my life with Jay my spirit was in pieces, mind in restless confusion and body flailing alone in sweat soaked sheets. I was all over the place, buying new clothes, driving fast while screaming along with my music. And dating as much as possible. I met men online at all kinds of web sites, they were all younger and they were all beautiful. It was light and things had been heavy for far too long. They only wanted me for my body and I hadn't felt that anyone had wanted my body in years. I colored my hair, began wearing very feminine clothes and rediscovered myself. Did sex with many men that I never knew their last names and could barely remember their first names make me feel better about myself, by now you know the answer: it sure as hell did! I had a fucking amazing time! It was so freeing to tell someone that they should come home with me and that they did.

There are all these images in the media that women have to be thin, tan, young, blond haired and blue eyed for a man to want you. It is all lies. That I was older was a turn on and that I knew and accepted my body made them want me even more. Looking back having sex with those twentysomething year old men had nothing to do with my ex, it had to do with me figuring out who I was without her. When I became an actively sexual human being again it was terrifying and glorious all at the same time. Men were a foreign concept too, I hadn't seen a penis in over 15 years, and I was clueless. I learned that men were understanding with these sorts of things. They're just happy they have a naked woman next to them attempting to bring them pleasure. I thrusted myself at them because they were nothing like my old life. So, I am grateful to all those arms, mouths and other parts of varying sizes for helping me find me. My escapades have made for entertaining stories to my married friends. They have lived vicariously through my tantalizing naked tales. Now that it has been a few years, I know that I chose every single one of those men because they were what I needed at the time.

A transformation happened while I was just trying to survive my divorce, I started not only liking myself but loving who I was. I enjoyed going for hikes in the forest alone, buying a kids pack at the movies (a little popcorn, not a monstrosity of a soda and a snack size bag of plain m&m's.) I took myself on a weekend spa/writing getaway.

Now I don't require the ego boost of the younger hot body. Through all my involvements of the flesh I've gone from a self-containing and restraining lesbian 1950's style wife to a world traveling adventurer and paramour of many. The most important one being myself.

I am grateful for the agony, harsh words, tears and feelings of being lost because I'm where I am today due to all of it. I am giddy about tomorrow. Looking back over the last four years I grew with more veracity and ferociousness than ever in my 40 years. I had some epic elevations and some plummeting collapses. I know that life will share higher and lower ones with me as well.

24

Wanderlust and Farewell Feelings

I question why things far away seem more special and thrilling then what I have in my town? I am thankful every day for where I live yet I yearn to see the unknown. The Pacific Ocean is a 15 minute walk from my house, yet the Mediterranean Sea leaves me speechless.

Why does life feel so much more open when I am alone somewhere I have never been surrounded by people I don't know? I do miss home when I am gone but only after about 2 weeks. I sometimes question if this is normal behavior. Then I quickly come to the conclusion that I don't care. I now revel in my untethered ways.

Numerous people I know are married or have children, a mortgage, many responsibilities and I really don't. If I could travel six months a year and be in my hometown of Santa Cruz, California the other remaining six months, that would be ideal. What exactly would I be doing during all of those months? I have no idea. My main traveling goal is to see the word while helping animals and people. I do need to have shelter, food, water, and life's essentials.

It's not about visiting it's about submerging my soul into where my body is for that moment, hour or evening. It's about losing and finding myself somewhere I've never been. I discovered that it is the not knowing what is around the corner that entices me above all else. I am insatiable for the discovery of new finds.

My eyes looked at a map of the world, all the countries in their different shapes and sizes and I wondered where to go next. What undiscovered adventures of my life were waiting for me to celebrate with them? What spices will set my tongue on fire or sweet berry scent will open up my mind? Is it a breeze from the Mediterranean or the Atlantic that will require a sweater to be placed over my shoulders by my own soft hands? Will I work with my strong small back muscles, my quick witted brain or both? How many languages will tickle off my tongue with ease when I am 80? Will I live to be 80?

This life of mine is about saying yes. It is about: goose bumps that went all the way up my arm; The dress shop that made me feel alive, like a famous fashion model; Soaring over the island of Yelapa hundreds of feet in the air only connected by a cord to the boat below; The adventure in the cave of the dragon that was over a million years old; Being in a music video and having my face be the icon people click on YouTube to see it.

My goal is that every person reading this book that has shared in my story will know however excruciating things have been for you, you can experience so much pleasure again in your life. You will be able to delight in it because of all of the suffering you have endured. One day the woe will be replaced by subtle and then full on exuberance.

If you don't ask, it is always a no. Say YES to life, what do you have to lose? Ask someone out, take yourself out, do something that challenges your comfort zone. It's your life, if you don't live it to the fullest, who will?

I refuse to look back on my life with regrets of things I didn't do. I plan on being a part of many soils of this planet, walking, running, skipping and dancing. There is a blossoming world out there and why can't we all see it? I know that I was born with privilege, a white girl child born in California in the United States to lower middle class mother and father in 1975. I never went to bed hungry, my parents read to me. I was told by my grandmother that I could be anything I wanted. I was good in school, creative and learned to respect my body that was never a size 2 with breasts that never fit into a training bra.

In my early twenties I rejected femininity, shaved my head, pierced my left eyebrow and didn't shave or wear makeup. I changed my name to one that had more significance to me than being named after a grandfather who preached hate instead of acceptance. When I rejected all of the things I thought I was supposed to be as a woman in America, and then chose to wear skirts and mascara, it was because that was the most honest expression of my Self.

I managed to break free from my self-imposed chains, all of the shoulds and what ifs dissolved into the background. At least on most days. I now walk calmly open into a fresh water pool of possibilities. The waves of ideas swirl around my feet, raising up, the deeper I delve. Each morning there is no longing for a better life. I am still practicing, but am a committed novice to the continued discovery of me. I don't want the process to ever finish. As long as I'm breathing on this planet, I will continue my self-excavating.

The assortment of lovers, affairs, friendships-with-benefits, friends and authentic loves educated me. I was seeking forgiveness of myself and they helped me unravel my own mystery. With every human and country, I discovered them as well as myself. The conclusion, I have been found. My soul is certain of it and most importantly I comprehend that I don't need to find my "other" or "better," half. I am not in search of another human being to complete me. When the time is perfect, I know I will meet her, my person, to run wild and free beside, but that time is not now.

All of the slogging through my murky clumps of torment transformed me. The sludge polished my rough edges and made me shiny as I tumbled. Who knew the gunk had miracles hidden inside of it.

So, this is where I leave you, in the knowing of being the love of my own life. I hope my story has encouraged you to be the love of your own life, too. It doesn't matter if you have a partner, kids, all kinds of love in your life, being your own love is just, if not more, important.

I sit, waiting for a plane with a new, lighter weight, red-wine colored backpack at my side. My latest solo trip, flying nonstop to Iceland, the land of ice and fire.

I know that is the perfect place for me to start my next adventure. Ice and fire, freezing and burning and everywhere in between I have felt and shared with you. Thank you for being my witness. I hope the pleasure hasn't all been mine.

25

Epilogue

Hello again! I finished writing this in 2017 and the story actually ended in 2015, the year I turned 40. Now, as I approach my 46th birthday, I am so excited to have this published! I realize, I was not ready to be vulnerable and open myself to people until I had some space from it all. Almost nine years after my separation/divorce, I have distance and can just be in gratitude. I had many years of confusion, sadness, anger and a fun, wild single life. I regret none of it and am also thrilled that I have met my person. My amazing love, Shawna and I have been together over two years. I am also expanding my love of writing to poetry, fiction and who knows what the future will bring!

I still believe in miracles and magic. (Wo)manfesting daily! Thank you so much for being a part of it all!

Joyfully,

Labris

About the Author

Labris Willendorf is a passionate, creative, femme adventurer. She has had travel articles published in Jubel and *How I Became The Love of My Life* is her first full length publication. Ms. Willendorf earned her Bachelor of Arts degree in Women's Studies from the University of California, Santa Cruz.

Ms. Willendorf is a feminist and equal rights activist. Traveling to places she has never experienced awakens her soul like nothing else. She is also thrilled to be at home with her amazing love, cook vegetarian meals and play with their rescue dog.

Ms. Willendorf is currently working on a novel, as well as writing poetry. She looks forward to traveling when it is safe and continuing to live each day in enthusiasm, gratitude and joy.